THE
PRIVATE
EYE
ANNUAL
1997
EDITED BY IAN HISLOP

"You fool – you forgot to get any gossip"

Published in Great Britain by
Private Eye Productions Ltd,
6 Carlisle Street, London W1V 5RG

©1997 Pressdram Ltd.
ISBN 1 901784 00 2
Designed by Bridget Tisdall.
Printed in England by
Ebenezer Baylis & Son Ltd, Worcester

2 4 6 8 10 9 7 5 3

THE PRIVATE EYE ANNUAL 1997

EDITED BY IAN HISLOP

UPFRONTERS

at Elton John's Fancy Dress Birthday Party

Adam Faith is having a **Sir Walter Raleigh** good time!! And **Elizabeth the First** has come Hurley to join in the hilarious fun!

Dawn French **Hardy** needs no introduction!! Particularly not to Joanna, who is having a Lumley time as **Stan**!? Yes, they're having an abfab night out as they join in the hilarious fun!

Richard and Judy meet their Waterloo as **Napoleon** and the **Duke of Wellington**! Yes it *is* tonight **Josephine** as the TV couple join in with the other celebrities in the hilarious fun!

Vinnie Jones is a revolting sight as **Spartacus**!! Look at him slaving away?! Perhaps he's going to tackle Elton from behind to add to the hilarious fun which everyone is having!!

David Bowie is the **Cowieboy** of the night!?! Ten-Gallon hats off to Ziggie Prairiedust as he joins in the hilarious fun!

Ned Sherrin is revolting as the Mexican rebel **Zapata**!! *(You've done this one. Ed.)* And who is stringing you along?! None other than Lady Ocharina Frost as gypsy queen **Carmen**! Or is it Anna Ford as **Mary Queen of Scots**?! No, I'll tell you who it is — it's Mariella Frostrup as **Tarzan's Jane**?! And actually, looking at my notes again, it might be Sir Robin Day as **Hopalong Cassidy**! Anyway, whoever it is, they are having hilarious fun in hilarious style at the decade's most hilarious *(You're fired. Ed.)*

Cherie to Edit Eye!

We are proud to announce that the next edition of Private Eye will be edited by Ms **Cherie Blair**, the distinguished QC and wife of the leader of the Labour Party, Mr Tony Blair.

Here is a taste of what you will read in the next Eye.

A Taxi Driver Writes

David Blunkelt (Cab No. 274):

"Blimey, see those trade unionists on the telly? They've got a nerve, 'aven't they? Going on strike and annoying the public? Know what I'd do when I got into power? String 'em up, it's the only language they understand.

And another thing. See them Euro's trying to tell us we can't give our kids a clip round the ear'ole? Blimey! Never did me no 'arm. I'd like to give 'em a good hidin'. It's the only language they understand, apart from French, German, Finnish and all that stuff.

I 'ad that Mrs Thatcher in the back of the cab once. What a wonderful woman, guv. An inspiration to us all.

Plus All your old favourites (Except Dave Spart who's too left wing) including:

✔ **Lord Gnome** – "Why I'm giving all my money to Tony Blair's New Labour Party."

✔ **The Glenda Slagg Profile** – "Tony Blair, dontcha love him?"

✔ **Literary Review** – Ken Follett's brilliant new novel, reviewed by Barbara Follett.

✔ **E.J. Thribb** – "So. Farewell then the Tories..."

All this and more in the next issue of "Cher-Eye", edited by the wife of our Prima Minister-in-waiting! Geddit?

SUPERGRASS WALKS FREE

New Scandal Breaks

by Our Legal Affairs Correspondent
Joshua Rozenbeard

One of the country's top criminals was today at liberty once more following his amazing let-off by Britain's legal system.

By any normal standards, Michael Howard should be paying his debt to society after being found guilty of releasing highly dangerous drug dealers onto the streets and dealing in massive amounts of low quality excuses (popularly known as "shit").

Super-arse

But it emerged yesterday that when caught red-handed in a blatant act of incompetence he gave the authorities the name of his associate, Justice Cocklecarrot of the Old Bailey. Said Howard:

"The Judge told me to let out these drug dealers. I had nothing to do with it. He's the one you should be talking to, officer, not me. Honest, let me go."

The public are, however, outraged that Howard has escaped yet again.

"You spoil that cat, Paul"

Jimmy Knapp General Secretary of P.M.T. (formerly A.S.L.E.E.P.) explains the latest move in the rail dispute.

Urr oberammergau geronimo step we gaily marie's wedding old macdonald had a happy meal FURTHER STOPPAGES INEVITABLE legoland at Windsor Longleat safari park jimmy shand neil shand REFRESHMENT BREAK eric cantonana shananana say goodbye white heather club leather club MANAGEMENT STICKING POINT ariadne auf naxos THREATS AND COERCION TOWARDS MY MEMBERS millennium tower norman foster mulholland falls gwyneth paltrow UNAVOIDABLE DISRUPTION bocaccio ruud gullit (continued throughout Autumn)

GOD'S FURY OVER "SENSATIONAL" BIOGRAPHY

by Our Religious Affairs Correspondent
Humphrey Carpenter of Nazareth

A cosmic row erupted last night over a new book entitled *The Bible*, based on tape-recorded interviews with God, in which he apparently attacks almost everybody who has ever lived.

Among the chief targets of his indiscretions were:

● **Adam** – *"a tremendous disappointment – charming but ineffectual."*
● **Eve** – *"an actress and schemer, though a lovely girl."*
● **Noah** – *"a bit wet – ha, ha, ha."*
● **Job** – *"whingeing old bore, always coming to me with his problems."*
● **Jezebel** – *"a bit of a tart, but a lovely girl."*
● **David and Jonathan** – *"they never really liked me, because I wasn't one of them.*

However, the Almighty's strongest criticism was apparently directed at the former Archbishop of Canterbury, the Rt. Rev. Robert Runcie, whom he described as "an indiscreet old woman who couldn't keep his mouth shut. He was always getting into trouble. But at least he had a good war."

Tape Recording Angel

Last night a spokesman for God was quick to deplore the revelations (particularly Chapters 12, 13, 14 and 15). He said that God had "only been speaking for background. He had made it clear that his remarks were not to be taken as Gospel."

He added "The Almighty was under the impression that nothing would be used until after his death, which was not likely to happen for some time."

"We decided to let him off with a warning this time!"

How It Works:
The Stealth Bomber

How Stealth looks on those Iraqi radar screens.

The Stealth bomber is the most sophisticated weapon in the US military arsenal. The US's state-of-the-art technology has developed a bomber so ingeniously designed that it can never be detected by either side. Even when it has attacked the target and delivered its payload, there is no visible sign that it has ever been there. Recently used in Iraq with great success. After waves of attacks by hundreds of Stealth bombers on Saddam's secret Command HQ, not even Hussein himself was aware that the attack had taken place and the buildings were still standing exactly as they were before.

Next Week: Have We Got Cruise For You – how the smart missile is so smart that it wins the US election without hitting anything.

MAXWELL CHRISTENING PHOTO

Look Kevin. He's got his grandfather's lies

THE BOOK OF BENJAMIN

Chapter 94

1. And lo Benjamin, who is called Netanyahu, ruled in the land of Israel.

2. And Benjamin said to the children of Israel: "Behold, I bring a rod of iron for the backs of Araf-ites and the Arab-ites.

3. "And when they see it they will shiver and shake like unto a Pomegranate in the early Frosts of Hebron.

4. "Then will the Araf-ites seek peace for hithertc they know it not in any meaningful sense."

5. Then the children of Israel clapped their hands and rejoiced even as if they hearkeneth to their entry in the song contest that is called Eurovision.

6. Even as when Wogan, that is called Tel, cometh forth and pronounceth "Israel nul points."

7. And then they rose up and went into the West Bank and pitcheth their tents in the lands where dwelleth the Arab-ites.

8. And the children of Israel crieth with one voice:

9. "This land is ours. It sayeth so in the Book of Begin and the Book of Shamir.

10. "So it must be true."

11. Then Benjamin spake again to the children of Israel, saying: "Lo! Let us dig up the tunnel of our ancestors, even the tunnel of our fathers and their fathers' fathers and their (Get on with it. God.)"

12. "Even the tunnel that goeth straight underneath the Holy Place of the Araf-ites."

13. And the people said unto themselves: "Good. This will really annoy the Araf-ites."

14. And they took up their spades and diggeth mightily under the rock until they came even underneath the temple of the ungodly.

15. Then Benjamin looked on his work and was pleased and saith to his wife Sarah:

16. "Verily, I am going on a long journey to tell the peoples of the world that I am a man of peace."

17. So he came even into Lon-don to see the leader of the Brittites, a man called John, Brother of Terry, Son of Major-Ball the Gnomemaker.

18. And it came to pass that even as Benjamin spake to John of the Dove of Peace, the Araf-ites took arms in their fury at the Tunnel of Benjamin.

19. And they hurled rocks and stones at the Sons of Israel.

20. And Arafat himself waxed wrath crying: "Wo unto Benjamin for he has broken his word unto me."

21. But Benjamin hearkeneth not and told the sons of Israel to get on with the smiting.

22. And they did so, smiting even three hundredfold of the Araf-ites.

23. But it was not all one way.

24. For this time the Araf-ites were armed even unto their teeth with guns given to them by Rabin, the Peacemaker.

25. And the Araf-ites did a bit of smiting themselves.

26. And they returneth an eye for an eye and a bullet for a bullet.

27. And the Children of Israel were sore amazed and muttereth amongst themselves: "Verily, this is not in the script (Surely 'scripture'? God)."

28. And there was great wailing and gnashing of teeth and firing of semi-automatics.

29. But Benjamin's heart was hardened and he crieth in a loud voice: "Let the Araf-ites do as they will. For I am a rock and I moveth not, even as the rocks stand in the place called Megido, that is Armageddon, which it will be if I have anything to do with it."

30. And the Children of Israel sang his praises by day and by night.

31. It was just like old times.

(To be continued)

NOW SHOWING

NOT emma

An amazing new film without Emma Thompson in it. And she didn't even write the screenplay. Not quite as good as the film with Emma in it but very similar to films with Emma in them. By Jane Austen who is very like Emma. NOT Emma – but with her Mum and her Sister.

"When first the cuckoo speak 'is mind, the Christmas catalogue bain't far behind"

IN THE COURTS

What You Missed When the Hamilton/Greer Libel Action Collapsed

Day 94: Guardian Newspapers vs Neil Hamilton & Ian Greed

Sir Robertson Jeffries QC: M'Lord, I should like to call my first witness — Mr Mohammed Al-Fayed, one of the greatest living Englishmen.

(At this point an odd-looking man of Egyptian origin entered the court with a Harrods Food Hall bag from which he extracted large wads of £20 notes which he proceeded to hand out to the Jury and the Judge)

Fayed *(for it is he)*: Just a little something for you from your old friend Mohammed.

Justice Cocklecarrot: This is most improper.

Fayed: Then go fuck yourself, you stuck-up fuckhead.

Sir Robertson: I do apologise profusely, my lord, for my witness's behaviour. He is new to this country and is not familiar with our ways. Now Mr Fayed will you tell the court what is your name?

Fayed: My name is Prince Mohammed Fayed Burlington-Smythe, the son of King Fayed the Magnificent, Ruler of the Seven Seas and Pharaoh of the Twelve Tombs.

Sir Charles Greyman: M'Lud, I submit on behalf of Mr Hamilton and Mr Greed that this is nothing but a pack of lies. The man before the court is none other than the notorious Alexandrian carpet bagger Mr Shufti Al-Kruk.

Fayed: You fucking bastard. I'll never give your Mr Hamilton another fucking penny.

Cocklecarrot: Mr Fayed, if there are any more of these unsavoury outbursts I shall have to charge you with contempt of court.

Fayed: That's all right boss. You can charge me what you like. I've got plenty of money.

(Mr Fayed at this point passed the Judge another bundle of notes)

Usher: Shall I mark this Bundle "B" your honour?

Cocklecarrot: I think it is time for luncheon.

Fayed: Good idea! Everyone come to the Ritz. It's all on me. Lotsa luvly girls! Plenty good jig-a-gig! Filthy postcard anyone?

(The case continued for several weeks)

Autumn Best-Sellers

1. Ned Sherrin's Diary
RADIO's Naughty Ned takes us through his daily round of celebrity interviews, theatrical anecdotes, large dinners and agreeable rentboys *(shurely 'restaurants'? Ed). (Luvvie Press £14.99)*

2. The Oxford Book of Ned Sherrin's Anecdotes
RADIO's Naughty Ned tells us some more of his sparkling anecdotes, many of them for only the hundredth time. Join in once more in Ned's ceaseless whirl of celebrity interviews, agreeable dinners and large rentboys *(shurely 'cheques'? Ed). (Trouserpress £19.99)*

3. Scratch Your Eyes Out by Ned Sherrin
RADIO's Naughty Ned's first foray as a novelist. Basil Twinky is a writer and radio presenter who inhabits a colourful world of celebrity interviews, theatrical anecdotes and five-star rentboys *(shurely 'hotels'? Ed).* Twinky moreover is a brilliant raconteur and the passage where he tells his story about Gertrude Stein and Ralph Richardson will leave you helpless with sleep. *(Random Cottage £48.99)*

5. Diary of a Nobody by Norris Norris
THE former Transport Minister, Norris Norris, takes us behind the scenes into the fascinating world of the Transport Ministry. His amazing account of the A372 bypass controversy is nearly as dull as everything else in the book. As broadcast by Radio Bore's "A Book at Sleeptime" and read very badly by the author himself. *(Vanity Press £7.75)*

CHANCELLOR WAS AT ST CAKES
Headmaster's rebuke to Major

by Our Education Staff **Lunchtime O'Levels**

AN ANGRY Mr Kipling, headmaster of the £35,000-a-term Midlands public school St Cakes (motto "Who pays, passes"), hit out last night at the Prime Minister for suggesting that Kenneth Clarke was a "state-school" boy.

"This is nonsense," he said, speaking from his book-lined study. "Clarke K. came to Cakes in 1953 on one of our Festival of Britain Assisted Bursaries. He was an outstanding pupil and Head of Jazz in the Lower Vth."

The proud headmaster showed me a yellowing copy of the school magazine, *The Cakeian*, showing a picture of the St Cakes' All-Stars Dixieland Foot-Tappers with the young "Jelly Roll" Clarke playing the trumpet. Next to him stood banjo-player C.J.P. Silvester-Smythe and tuba player E.F.B. "Hotlips" Hoffnung Minor.

Exceedingly Bad Jazz

"We are proud of the fact that the chancellor of this country was once treasurer of the Cakes' Keynes Society where he presented a paper apologising for losing all the Society's money on a horse at the 3.00 at Haydock Park."

Mr Kipling has written to the Prime Minister asking for a written apology.

LINE DANCING GNOMES £ IS A YARD.

SCOTT FAILS TO REACH SOUTH COAST

by Our Antarctic Staff **Lunchtime O'Ates**

THE LEGENDARY British explorer Sir Nicholas Scott last night failed in his epic bid to walk the 200 yards from the Irish Embassy party to his hotel on the South Coast in Bournemouth.

He had set off fully prepared with provisions, carrying inside his stomach ten cases of Guinness and three bottles of Irish Whiskey.

But very soon he felt under the weather, and his vision was distorted by a blizzard of swirling buildings that seemed to fly around him.

He pitched base camp on the side of the road and then unwisely wandered off. He fell down a pavement and was found dead drunk in the gutter.

His last words on leaving the party were: "I'm passing out now. I may be some time."

Sir Nicholas Scott is 70 proof.

GLENDA LA SLAGGE

Fleet Street's Prime Rubbish

● GEOFF BOYCOTT!? Donchaluvhim? Well all the other gals do apparently!? (Geddit?) OK so he bashes up the odd bird but you can count on it that when Geoff does it he does so with grace and skill and style and chooses just the right minute to hit out!?! Yes, you can be sure that Boycs takes a run only when hubby is coming down the drive and he'll have a solid defence when the maiden bowls him over in the tabloids?! Good old Geoff!!

○ GEOFF BOYCOTT!? What a bastard!? Who does this Yorkshire oik think he is?! Casa-bleedin'-nova?!!! Bashanova-the-head more likely?! (Geddit?!) If I were his bird (which thank Gawd I aint!?!) it would be me who would pad up and buy a helmet?!! Why don't we all just *Boycott* him?!! (Geddit?!?!) Bugger off back to the Referendum Party with all the other lunatics and wierdos!?!

■ *HATS OFF to Richard Branson!? The Roaming-Handed Romeo of the skies!? No wonder the girls are queuing up at Beardie's check-in desk!? And you can betcha they're not virgins (Geddit?). I say what Britain needs is more hands-on managers like Big Dick?! (Geddit?!)*

● ISN'T HE disgusting? Richard Branson I mean, stoopid!? With his filthy pullover and scruffy beard he looks like a dirty old man — which he is!? You want Auntie Glenda's opinion?! You're virgin on the obscene mate! Take off in one of your silly balloons and don't come back!

○ TALKING of silly beards, seen Trevor Nunn's *Twelfth Night*?! It won't run until the thirteenth?! (Geddit?) Sorry, Luvvie?! (Geddit!)

○ HERE they are — Glenda's Bonfire Bangers!

CHRISTOPHER BROCKLEBANK-FOWLER — he doesn't know what party to join — so he can come round and join mine?!

SENATOR DOLE — OK, so you had a mistress 30 years ago?? Wanna try your luck again? (Geddit?)

ALEXANDER McQUEEN — Queen by name, Queen by nature?! But that's alright with me!? Any man who designs the "Bumster" must be a complete arse!? Geddit!?

Ciaoooooee!

Notes & Queries

QUESTION: Why are new shirts full of pins? — *Mrs Ludmilla Netanyahu, Stoke Newington*

□ THIS custom dates back to ancient Athens when a group of laundry women sought their revenge on the lecherous King Pentos by filling his shirts with poisoned pins. Pentos pulled on the shirt and was immediately pricked to death. The incident was incorporated into the famous Greek Drama "The Laundrywomen" by the Tragedian Stassinopoulos. — *Professor Reginald Van Heusen, Pinner, Middlesex.*

□ I TAKE issue with Professor Van Heusen on the pin question. This is I am sorry to say yet another consequence of our membership of the EU. Under directive 747382/b British shirts are obliged to contain a minimum of 15 pins solely in order to protect the grossly inefficient Spanish Pin Industry. — *C.J.P. Booker, Dunfishin, Dorset.*

QUESTION: Why do flies buzz? — *Rev. Winifred Winnifreth, Wiltshire.*

□ THE male fly has a special second tongue which vibrates at 9 million VRMs per second to produce a constant humming noise which attracts the female fly and also people with rolled-up copies of the Guardian. — *Sir David Attenborough, Room 101, BBC.*

QUESTION: Is it true that the first light bulb was square? — *Kevin Rusbridger, Farringdon Road, London.*

□ YES. The original "Luminous Lighting Chamber" was invented in 1899 by a British scientist, Sir Clive Sinclair-Stevenson, an eccentric recluse who also devised the world's first electrically heated trousers. The lighting chamber was indeed square, made with panes of glass from Sinclair-Stevenson's greenhouse, and lit a small room for at least three seconds before exploding. It was in such an accident that Stevenson, wearing the electric trousers, was blown into his fish pond where he met an untimely death. His idea was later pirated by the German-American entrepreneur Otto Von Lightbulb. — *A.P. Rushton, curator of the National Light Bulb Museum, Osram House, Osram-on-Trent, Staffs.*

NEXT WEEK: Answers please: Can fleas swim? Is it true that Beethoven had a wooden leg? What does the 'N' stand for in A.N. Wilson?

"Isn't my bath full yet?!?"

A Doctor writes

AS a Russian Doctor, I am often asked by President Yeltsin: "Am I dead?"

The simple answer is: "Yes — or 'Da' to give it its full Russian name — but we can't tell anyone."

If you feel you are suffering from a case of Death Syndrome, or, as we doctors call it, *Mortalis kremlinus vodkosis abnormalis*, then you are advised to stay in Lebed.

© *World Copyright Pravdeye*

"He won't be long – he's just putting on his face"

SODOM ATTACK
God asked for apology

by Our Biblical Staff
Sodom Hussein and
John Selwyn-Gomorrah

Tuesday, 1000 BC

GAY rights organisations throughout the ancient world have launched the strongest possible protest at "an unprovoked homophobic assault on the popular cities of the plain known as Sodom and Gomorrah".

The two cities were reportedly completely wiped out by a massive dawn bombardment of fire and brimstone leaving everyone dead.

Thought for the Day of Judgement

Said a spokesman for the progressive Gay and Lesbian Pre-Christian Movement: "This is typical of the reactionary Old Testament approach that we have come to expect from Jehovah."

WORLD'S MOST WANTED WOMAN WALKS FREE

by Our BBC Staff **'Call'** Nick Dross

THE world's least-wanted television presenter, Enid Rancid, was cleared yesterday by an internal BBC report after being accused of "fixing the evidence" in a documentary about a nursing home.

The accusation was brought against her by fellow BBC employee John Wareishenow and proved conclusively that Enid was a manipulative and dishonest broadcaster who should be sacked at once.

Whitewash City

The BBC agreed, but said that in her defence it had to be made clear that Enid made a lot of cheap programmes full of sentimental rubbish which people quite liked even if they weren't true.

Sir Pigland Blind is 94.

You need a heart by-pass

Make it a double…

Those Papal Front Runners In Full

Who will take over the Vatican's No.1 hot-seat?

1. Cardinal Hume *(Britain)*
2. Cardinal Sin *(Philippines)*
3. Bonking Bishop Wright *(somewhere in Wapping)*
4. General Lebed *(Russia)*
5. Sister Wendy Beckett *(White City)*
6. Christina Odone *(Daily Telegraph)*
7. St Norman of Stevas *(Westminster)*
8. St James Goldsmith *(Mexico)*
9. St Gerald of Adams *(Ireland)*
10. Father Ted *(Channel 4)*
11. Father Ted *(Repeat)*

LOVE ROMP VIDEO A HOAX

by Our Hoax Staff **Stewart 'Borman' Stevens** and
Hugh 'Hitler's Diary' Very-Ropey (now known as Lord Paul Dacre)

A SENSATIONAL set of shock pictures published yesterday in the daily press was a complete fabrication by a team of very clever hoaxers, we can reveal.

The pictures purported to show John Major and Lady Thatcher engaging in intimate displays of affection in their hideaway conference centre in Bournemouth.

SHOCK

The couple are seen kissing, holding hands and whispering in each other's ears.

At one point Lady Thatcher is wearing nothing but a blue suit and a handbag, while Major sports only a grey suit and a pair of glasses.

But we can reveal that these pictures are nothing less than a fake, designed to hoodwink the British electorate into thinking that Lady Thatcher likes Mr Major.

The pictures are believed to be the work of a sinister, Ulster-born black propagandist, known in intelligence circles only as "Doctor Mawhinney".

HO-HO-HOAX

Last night an expert who had examined the pictures for several seconds told us: "These pictures should not have fooled anyone for a moment.

"You have only to look at the expression on the woman's face to see that she is acting a part.

"The man pretending to be the prime minister is even more unconvincing."

ON OTHER PAGES: Those Love-Romp Pix That Wouldn't Fool A Three-Year-Old 2-94

"This is Mr McKenzie – he's going to give a short talk on his work with the National Film Board of Canada"

SUN REVEALED AS 'HOAX'

by **Monty Video**,
Our Man In Uruguay

TODAY we can reveal that a black-and-white publication which for 25 years has been purporting to be a newspaper is in fact a gigantic hoax perpetrated on the public by a sinister Australian-born lunatic.

It now turns out that, after five minutes of investigation, the Sun has never been a newspaper at all.

It is merely a collection of pictures of women in their underwear accompanied by exhortations to vote Conservative by various clapped-out old hacks.

FULL STORY — page 94

Michelin Men Behaving Badly

10 THE INDEPENDENT
AT 10

Over the past 10 years the Indescribablyboring has brought you some of the most boring stories ever to appear in British journalism. Do you remember?

● 1986. Andreas Whittam-Strobes investigates a new threat to Britain's Cheese Industry.

● 1988. "The Lymeswold Saga". Andreas Whittam-Strobes begins a ten-week analysis of Britain's cheese crisis.

● "Say Cheese". Godfrey Hodgson looks at the link between the Conservative Party and the all-powerful Cheese Lobby.

● 1992. Alexander Chancellor launches the new-look Independent Magazine with black-and-white photos of Welsh cheeses, especially taken by Lord Snowdon.

● 1993. Stephen Glover re-launches the Sunday Independent with award-winning headline HARD CHEESE, MRS THATCHER, a fearless exposé of Tory cheese (shurely 'sleaze'? Ed).

● 1994-1996. Millionaire David Montgomery sacks everyone.

(That's enough highlights. Ed.)

From The Referendum Bunker

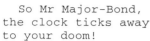

Bulletin No 94

Achtung!

So Mr Major-Bond, the clock ticks away to your doom!

And still you go off to the seaside and pretend that all is well. You fool!

That attractive woman who was all over you at the Conference Hall, Maggie Galore.

You thought she had fallen for your masculine charms, nicht wahr?

Oh Mr Bond, you disappoint me once again. You are so easily tricked.

Have you never heard of a double-agent? Maggie Galore is working only for one master in this game. Me! Sir Golden Syrup!

And now, Mr Bond, I have another little surprise for you. Carla, show in our new friend.

(Gina Lollobrigida lookalike in traditional Zulu

leather mini-skirt ushers in portly Scottish playboy in yellow hard hat)

I think you remember the former Chief Fund Raiser for your Conservative Party, Lord McAlpine.

Yes, Mr Major-Bond, he is just the latest of the constant stream of defectors to my ever-growing

army of Marmite soldiers.

So much better to be on the winning side, isn't it, Mr Bond. But you will never know!

Show our visitor your little party trick, Oddbob.

(The Lord McAlpine takes off hard hat and hurls it across underground cavern at swarthy greek waiter who is decapitated...)

Carla, remove what is left of poor Mr Taki and throw the remains to Mr Aspinall's killer giraffes.

He did not duck in time. Let it be a lesson to you, Mr Bond. This is what happens to those who do not get out of my way.

Goodbye Mr Bond. As always, I have so enjoyed our little talk. Start the countdown Carla.

(Sultry temptress, who is now wearing one-piece PVC bikini and white thigh-length boots, activates giant nuclear time-bomb due to explode if Britain joins the Single European Currency)

Issued by the Referendum Party of Great Britain

Room No 4013, Dorchester Hotel, London

(The theme tune this time is adapted from J.S. Bach's Goldfinger Variations)

A Doctor writes

AS A Doctor, I am often asked: "Doctor, what's wrong with me?" The simple answer is: "I haven't got time to tell you. I'm too busy writing a piece for the Daily Telegraph."

What happens is that the doctor is suffering from verbal diarrhoea, or 'Dalrymple's Syndrome', as it is known in the medical profession.

When asked by newspapers to write on any subject from the Single European Currency to the Scotland/Estonia football match, the doctor is unable to say "No".

The doctor then has to do night shifts as well as an 80-hour week, and this results in the doctor's column being extremely tired indeed.

If you find your doctor is writing too much, you should seek a second opinion piece in the Times.

© *Doctor Theodore Le Stuttaford.*

Now on Referendum Video

DAY OF THE JACKASS

Edward Fox is the Jackass, the ruthless deadly actor who is a master of disguise. One minute he is Edward VIII, the next he is Edward VIII again.

This time however he is hired by a mysterious group of Neo-Lunatics to terminate the Prime Minister.

Will he miss again?

Cast in full

The Jackass	. . . . . **Edward Fox**
Monsieur "G"	. . . **Charles Grey**
John Major	. . . . **Michael Caine**

"Hello, Mrs Turner – can Michael come out on the piss today?"

It's so easy!!!

Just pop out of the House of Commons, put out your hand and hop on a bus company! Hey presto! Within seconds you're on your way to becoming a millionaire!

Steve Norris says:

"It's as easy as hopping on a bird! One minute I was in charge of bus deregulation: the next minute I was running the buses! All on the board! Hold on tight to your money, because I'm trying to get it. Next stop the bank!"

Issued by The Capitalist Bus Co. plc

(Prop. S. Norris MP)

The Baron Leaves

Coming soon from the world's most prolific romantic novelist

by Barbara Cartland

LOVELY young widow Raine Spencer (78) is captivated by the dashing but heartless Baron von Hardup (62). Her mother, the wise, beautiful, young 93-year-old novelist with the body of a 16 year old, warns her daughter of the perils of the match.

"He is nothing but a worthless adventurer trying to cash in on someone's wealth and fortune," she says.

"That's why we're so well suited," Raine counters.

In the end her mother's words come back to haunt her as the wicked Baron shows his darker side…

Pills and Booze

(surely 'Mills and Boon'? Ed.)

Romantic Fiction At Its Worst

CHUNNEL FIRE BLAMED ON 'RUBBISH'

by Our Conflagration Staff
Mohamed Al-Fire and Michael Coal

THE cause of the huge Channel Tunnel blaze was last night identified as the vast containers of unsold copies of the humorous magazine *Punch*.

It is understood that the copies had been returned from France after an attempt to give them away to lorry drivers blockading roads had failed.

Millions of copies had thus been tightly packed into special containers for transportation back to England, but it is believed that angry French readers, incensed by the poor quality of the product, may well have set fire to the material before the train entered the tunnel.

Said one expert who examined the wreckage: "It was a disaster waiting to happen. Sooner or later someone was bound to set fire to these copies."

Yesterday, however, emergency services were blamed for the speed of their response to the fire.

"They were far too quick to put the fire out," said a Chunnel spokesman. "We are now left with a soggy mass that will take years to clear up."

Peter MacKay is Fayed.

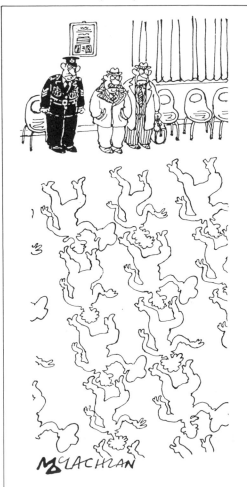

"I understand the Press are already calling it 'The Great Line-Dance Massacre'…"

Tonight's TV Highlights BBC

7.00 The Cone Men: real-life drama documentary which follows the 6-man M25 Cone Squad as they race into action to shut off the A23 Gatwick interchange following the breakdown of an HGV on the hard-shoulder. Led by Cone Commander Bill "Billy" Bixworth.

8.00 The Para Vets: real-life drama documentary showing the work of the Blue Cross crack Emergency Response Unit, led by Senior Paravet Officer Karen Fieldgate. Tonight's gripping episode follows Karen's team as they are helicoptered in to rescue a pet goldfish from up a tree.

9.00 The Lift Boys: new series. Michael Buerk introduces real-life reconstructions of incidents involving people being trapped in lifts. Tonight's episode centres on five businessmen caught between Floors 1 and 2 of the Cardiff Exhibition Centre. Will "Taffy" Teflon and his expert team of Elevator Rescue specialists manage to get them out in time for the important sales conference?

10.00 Spiderwatch UK: new series. Nick Ross introduces real-life reconstructions of the vital work of the Manchester arachno-busters. Tonight an Oldham widow panics when she finds a spider in her bath and calls in Pete "Scully" Fishwick and the squad. Later they are called out again on a false alarm, when a teenager thinks she has seen a spider underneath her bed.

11.00 Baggage Cops: Jeremy Paxman introduces new drama series based on the work of Gatwick Airport's elite luggage police. Led by former top Scotland Yard detective Charlie "Trolley" Catchpole, their job is to keep Europe's fourth busiest airport free from suitcase gridlock. Tonight panic breaks out when a passenger's golfbag on Flight BA725 from Amsterdam jams the notorious Carousel 3. Will the baggage cops get it moving, in time for the passenger to make his onward connection to Oman? *(That's enough TV. Ed.)*

TOGETHER AGAIN

I'm afraid I'm a public school Tory, mum

Welcome to the Labour Party

The Book of Benjamin

Chapter 94

1. And it came to pass in the days when Benjamin that is called son of Net-an-ya-hu was ruling over Israel, that he went up even unto Jerusalem.

2. And in the part of that city that lieth towards the east, Benjamin saw many tents, wherein dwelt the Arafites, the Hamasites and all the other ites that make up the tribes of the enemies of the children of Israel.

3. Then Benjamin waxed wroth in his heart, even as the porcupine waxeth wroth when it spieth the desert dog coveting its egg that it might eat of it unto itself.

4. Even in this wise did Benjamin that is called Net-an-ya-hu become jolly batey.

5. And he cried out to the children of Israel, saying Jerusalem, the holy city, is our city, even as it hath been foretold by Moses and all the prophets.

6. (For it is indeed one of the great coincidences of this book that the prophets have always foretold whatever thing it is that suiteth the case best at the present time.)

7. Yet now this holy place hath been defil-ed by the tents of the Philistines *(surely "Palestinians". Ed.)*

8. And Benjamin commanded the children of Israel to rise up and to go forth from the city, even unto the hill that is called Har-Homa, which is to say the place of residential development;

9. And there he commanded them to build many attractive, low-rise chalet-style homes, each with swimming pool and panoramic view of the Holy City (call Netanyahu Developments Plc, no relation, on 01746-7121 or, via the Internetanyahu, benhomes@jehovah.smiting.co.Israel).

10. And then the voice of A-ra-fat was heard in the land, even he that weareth the towel upon his head, and spake these words.

11. Benjamin, son of Net-an-ya-hu, hearken unto me. If the children of Israel lay so much as one stone upon another, we shall pick up the stones and cast them back at you, even an hundredfold.

12. And in the land of Us, that is called A-mer-ica, they looked upon these things and saw that they were not good.

13. And he that was king of the Amer-ican-ites, he that was called Clint-stone, summoned Benjamin even unto the house that is white, and instructed him that he must call off the dozers of bull and still the mixers of cement.

14. But Benjamin the son of Netanyahu hardened his heart, saying "What I have spoken, I have spoken. For I am the Lord's anointed, by a majority of 0.01 percent, and therefore whatsoever I sayeth, I sayeth."

15. And shortly afterwards the smiting began, as per usual.

NEXT WEEK: How Sara, the wife of Benjamin, appeareth on the cover even of the Telegraph magazine, showing her golden calves and telling it like it isn't.

POETRY CORNER

In Memoriam
Mastermind, **the BBC Television Quiz**

So. Farewell
Then
Mastermind.

You have
Started.

And now
You have
Finished.

   E.J. Thribb (17½ and no passes)

In Memoriam
Sir John Junor

So. Farewell
Then John
Junor. Columnist
And Editor.

What was
Your catchphrase?

I think
We should
Be told*.

      E.J. Thribb (17½)

Poet's Footnote*: These final lines are intentionally ambiguous. I appear to be asking what Sir John's catchphrase was, but this is what it was — i.e. I think we should be told. (E.J.T.)*

In Memoriam Jacques Cousteau

So. Farewell
Then Inspector
Clouseau.

Star of
The Pink Panther
Films.

Keith is
Not sure I
Have got this
Right.

     E. Jacques Thribbeau
     (17½ feet underwater)

In Memoriam: Marje Proops, the Doyenne of Agony Aunts

Dear Marje,
What is it
Like
Being dead?

Have you
Any advice?

These are
Questions
That even
You

Cannot answer.

By the
Way.

So.
Farewell
Then.

E.J. Throobs (17½)

In Memoriam: Lines Written On The Death Of Pamela Harriman 1872-1997

So. Farewell
Then Pamella
Bordes (surely 'Harriman'? Ed).
Courtesan extraordinaire.

You were "linked"
To almost
Every famous man
Of this century.

It says on your tombstone
"Now she is sleeping".
But it does not say
Who with.

E.J. Thribb (17½)

In Memoriam: Tiny Tim

So. Farewell
Then, Tiny
Tim.

Once you
Tiptoed through the
Tulips.

But now
You are
Pushing up the
Daisies.

E.J. Thribb (17½)

EDINBURGH FESTIVAL

DANCE

"Elvis — The Ballet". The internationally renowned Dance company of Zagreb tell the story of Elvis Presley reset in 15th Century Russia at the Court of Czar Zsa Gabor. Elvis is ingeniously danced by prima ballerina Olga Maitlandoff.
The Royal Caledonian Free Hall, 7.30pm (Venue No. 1,275)

FILM

"The Vomit Boys". World premiere of Gus McDuff's touching rite of passage tragi-comedy telling the story of three heroin-addicted HIV patients who go on a trip to EuroDisney. Winner of the coveted Palme Olive at the Haiti Festival de Cinéma.
The Old Railway Museum, 8.00pm (Venue No. 3,462)

COMEDY

"Slabb and Bucket". Michael Slabb and Rick Bucket, the stars of Channel 5's late night stand-up newcomers' show "Give Us 5!", consolidate their growing reputation as the most innovative comedians

performing on the fringe today. The show includes their famous Star-Trek sketch and the highly controversial Buying-Bananas-in-Supermarket-Routine.
"I laughed and laughed" — Nicholas McJongh, Scots and Scotsmen
St Jaspan's Church, 2.30pm (Venue No. 6,532)

CHILDREN

"Romeo and Juliet". The acclaimed Puppet Theatre of Ontario present their all-moose version of Shakespeare's tragedy. Complete with unforgettable specially written songs including: "Blue Moose" and "Can't Help Loving That Moose of Mine".
The Prince's Street Library, 4.00pm (Venue No. 25,378)

ART

"The Sandwich As Symbol". First ever exhibition of sandwiches from railway stations around the world, assembled by Austrian multi-media artists Gottlieb von Sarnie and Preta Manger. "This extraordinary triumph dazzles the eye and assaults the nose with a binary ocular and olfactorial brilliance that gives the sandwich a supreme cultural resonance. The black bread, yellow yak-meat and bright red peppers of the Istanbul Double Decker Sizzler will remain with me my whole life" — Richard Dorment, Daily Telegraph
The National Gallery of Scotland, all day (Venue No. 178,402)

(That's enough Edinburgh. Ed.)

DUCHESS SUFFERING FROM ME SYNDROME

PEOPLE close to the Duchess of York reckon that she has been suffering from what is commonly known as the ME syndrome. The symptoms normally manifest themself in the victim in the following ways: always talking about themselves; courting maximum personal publicity via the media; and selling exclusives to Hello! magazine.

The result is that everyone around the Duchess grows very tired (of her), and wants to drop off every time her name is mentioned. Said a spokesman for the Duchess: "Apparently, there is only one known cure for this ailment — a holiday. The only snag is that she will have to make another 50 personal appearances to be able to afford one."

MEDICAL BRIEFING

Dr Thomas Stuttaford

Is it ME again?

YES, sadly it is. What usually happens in these cases is that you have to read even more pieces by ME, as soon as the news breaks that anyone has got any disease and *(cont. p. 94)*

GIACOMETTI'S NIGEL LAWSON

Memorial Service

A service of thanksgiving for the life and work of Mrs "Marje" Proops was held at St Brides Church, Ludgate. The Rev J.C. Flannel officiated. The following hymns were sung: "Riders in the Sky" (F. Lane), "Shrimp Boats Are A-Comin' In" (A. Cogan) and "Sexual Healing" (M. Gaye).

Miss Glenda Slagg read "How to Keep Hubby Happy in Bed" from Chapter 7 of the *Daily Mirror Book of Sex Tips* (editor M. Proops).

Mr Lunchtime O'Booze related an anecdote concerning Mrs Proops, her long-time lover and a parrot who could only say "Cor! What a big one!".

A tribute from the late Robert Maxwell was read out by Mr Joe Haines.

Those present included a number of senior Agony Consultants including Ms Molly Barmy, Ms Claire de Looney, Ms Linda Blimey and Ms Jackie Tacky.

The reception was held at El Winos.

Tutankhamen Behaving Badly

EMPEROR BOGAZZA DEAD

by Our Man in the Congo
King Conga

Gazzaville, Tuesday

ONE OF the most unpleasant and violent men of the twentieth century, the Emperor Bogazza, has died at the age of 28.

His short and brutal career was marked by a series of bestial acts culminating in a ferocious attack on his wife, the Empress Shezza.

Bogazza, a man of humble birth on the River N'Tyne, came to believe he was all-powerful and indestructible. He dressed in leopard-skin suits, dyed his hair yellow and would strike out in drunken rages at anybody who came near him. In the end he believed he was God and lived *(cont. p.94)*

OTHER DEATHS

TOMMY LAWTON, Footballer and Gentleman.

Deirdre Spart, Co-Chair of the Lesbian Feminist Alternative Committee of Selectors of the England Football Team

IT IS totally sickening to my mind the way the England capitalist soccer bosses have once again totally condoned the patriarchal violence perpetrated by so-called Gazza against his partner thereby endorsing the pathological woman-hater Gascoigne as a role model for millions of infantile so-called men whose only emotional response is one of systematic brutalised Fascist repressionism against all women thus once again proving that soccer is not a genuine working-class cultural artefact but a tool of capitalist masculinism as Julie Burchill has written in her seminal classic *Scoring Girls* published by the Ravendyke Press which should be made compulsory reading for all schools *(cont p. 94)*

GAZZA'S SOCK'ER TIPS Part 94

1. CONTROL
Drink 20 pints of lager and lose it completely.

2. TACKLING
Tackle someone female and weak about an imaginary slight.

3. FOOTWORK
Don't forget to use your feet as well as your hands and your head. A good kicking needs all your skills.

4. BALANCE.
Remember your bank balance and apologise to the press afterwards.

5. DRIBBLING
Give a press conference and dribble on about guilt, shame, remorse, counselling, therapy, and getting your place in the England team back.

NEXT WEEK: *Boycott's Guide to Opening the Beating.*

PETER McLIE
THE COLUMN THAT PACKS HIS BAGS AT PUNCH

HERE are my predictions for next month's budget. I forecast that the chancellor will either:
a) Raise taxes
or
b) Bring them down.
Whichever happens I will eat my hat if I am wrong.

◻ SOMEONE has stolen all the leaves from the tree in my garden. I have rung the police to tell them but they have done nothing. The burglar was in such a hurry that he left most of them on the ground.
Surely it is not beyond the wit of our boys in blue to nab the offenders? Isn't life dandy?

◻ HAS anyone read the column above? Not very interesting was it? I blame the papers for failing to provide anything interesting in them!

◻ HAS anyone seen what was in the paper yesterday? Not very interesting was it? Particularly not for people looking for ideas for columns.

I HAVE a new idea for making a lot of money very quickly. It's called the sack. You get it if you're no good at your job but if you're canny you make sure that you get a vast pay-off in order to get rid of you quickly. Isn't life 180 grandee?

"Look, I must go – autumn is my busy time"

SCOTT'S TRAGIC END AFTER FAILING TO REACH SOUTH KEN

THE epic journey of one gallant Englishman has ended in tragic failure, it has been reported.

The legendary Sir Nicholas Scott has failed by only a few votes to become the first extremely drunk Englishman to be selected as MP for Kensington and Chelsea.

For months Scott battled against the odds in his ill-fated attempt to reach the poll without the use of legs.

Yesterday, as a nation mourned, hundreds of tributes poured in from colleagues and friends.

Said one Cabinet minister, "Don't quote me, old boy, but he had it coming to him."

(Reuters)

That University Challenge Rout in full

BIRK

(Silly music and studio applause)

Paxperson *(for it is he):* Tonight our contestants are Blackstone College, London, named after the legendary Tessa Blackstone, and the University of Neasden (formerly the North Circular Polytechnic).

(Buzzer sounds from Wayne Einstein of Neasden)

Einstein: The answers to the first 30 questions are: Beethoven's opus 131, Zimmelmann's Third Law, the anacrobrytic bone, Beach Boys 1963, James Chuter-Ede, 135 for 6 declared and 418-2, the Elder Pliny, Ford Madox Ford *(continues in similar vein for 20 minutes).*

Paxmachine: Look, I'm going to offer the next question only to Blackstone, who are now 550 points behind. Blackstone, what are your names? And remember, no conferring…

All: Er…

(Buzzer sounds from Einstein of Neasden)

Einstein: Simon Beard, Mike Dim, Sandra Cardigan and Danny Dandruff.

Paxvobiscum: Correct. So the final score is Neasden 786 and Tessa Blackstone minus-20…

(Silly music plays. Ends)

ON OTHER PAGES

Why Oh Why Are Today's Students So Ignorant Apart From The Ones From Neasden? asks **Paul Johnson**, who didn't see the programme.

WALLPAPER

MALE PATTERN BALDNESS

CLINTON'S SPIN DOCTOR GIVES BLAIR TEN-POINT VICTORY PLAN

by Our Political Staff **Norman Mailer on Sunday**

GEORGE Stephanotaloton-topalis flew into London today to present Labour leader Tony Blair with a ten point plan for "Victory — the Clintstone way". These are his radical recommendations that will sweep Britain's top social-democrat into the White House.

1. Cherie to die hair blonde and put hand in till of law firm.

2. Tony to take sax lessons.

3. Tony to take sex lessons from assorted bimbos including Gennifer Flowers.

4. Mandelson to commit suicide in mystery sleaze row.

5. Tony to be sued for sexual harassment by Clare Short.

6. Blair children to be re-christened Islington, Highbury, Barnett and Neasden.

7. Blair to run against someone useless. *(He's already got that bit. Ed.)*

8. Blair to hire myself at great expense.

9. Er…

10. That's it.

THAT CLINTSTONE ACCEPTANCE SPEECH IN FULL

Mah fellow Americans *[takes out huge bag of onions]*. This is a great day for Hillary, Chelsea and I. We stand before you, in the presence of God, to give thanks for our own humility in the face of this overwhelming victory for myself. We have won that gunfight at the OK Corral. We have crossed the Alamo into the 21st century. Together, we have gone boldly where no man has gone before. We have made that bridge in Madison County. We have built that bridge over troubled waters. We have gone a bridge too far. So help us God. So let us go forward on the highway of hope. Route 66, where I get my kicks. Yes, sirree. That old deadwood stage is a-comin' on over the hill. And the corn is as high as an elephant's eye. Oh, say, can't you see, by the dawn's early light. Yabbadabbadole…

NATIONAL ASSOCIATION OF SPIN DOCTORS

THIS IS NOT A DOOR

RGJ

Tributes to Comrade Birt flow in from all over BBC

Reprinted from the BBC House Magazine Birts & Birtmen

A 59-MINUTE standing ovation was accorded to the Great Helmsman, Comrade Kim Il Birt, by hundreds of thousands of loyal BBC workers on the occasion of the unveiling of Comrade Birt's Five-Year Plan For The Re-Organisation Of Management Structures And Corporate Directorates.

The proceedings were opened with a two-hour-long speech from Comrade John Simpson of the Foreign Affairs Unit, who praised the Great Leader's unswerving devotion to the Three Principles of Blandism-Birtism.

These principles, Comrade Simpson reminded his smiling co-workers, were:

1. Continual revolution in every department of the Corporation at all times.

2. Permanent stability through structural consolidation at the management-production interface.

3. Permanent employment of Myself at enormous salary commensurate with my status as Very Important Foreign Correspondent.

Wyatt Twerp

Comrade Simpson then attacked the "malicious hyenas and running dogs of the media who have dared to criticise the farsighted policies and actions of the Great Communicator, Our Beloved Comrade Birt."

Comrade Simpson's contri-bution was followed by a three-hour speech from Comrade Will Wyatt, the veteran Party ideologue and Grand Controller of the Internal Directorates.

Comrade Wyatt reminded his audience of the incredible achievements of Birtism, which had made the BBC what it was today.

He singled out for praise the following heroes of the Birtist Revolution:

● Comrade **Esther Rantzen**, for her fearless exposure of innocent people.

● Comrade **Peter Jay**, for his fearless exposition of the finer points of economic and monetary union.

● Comrade **Barry Norman**, for his fearless wry look at this week's New Releases.

● Comrade **Desmond Lynam**, for his fearless and revolutionary introductions to *Sportsnight*.

● Comrade **Christopher Evans**, Leader of the Birtist Youth Movement, for his fearless promotion of himself and for his tireless assault on the outmoded shibboleths of reactionary Auntie-ist bourgeois broadcasting under the slogan "Fart If You Think My Salary Should Be Trebled".

Comrades Behaving Badly

Comrade Yentob then took the floor and spoke for five hours on the theme of Comrade Birt's achievements in keeping him in his job.

Never before *(contd. p. 94)*

WAR CRIMINAL TOO SENILE TO ANSWER CHARGES

by Our Legal Staff **Joshua Rozenbeard**

AN elderly man living alone in Salisbury has been discharged after accusations of war crimes in the European Theatre between 1970 and 1974.

Edward Grosserawitz, 89, looked bewildered as leading prosecutor Sir James "Achtung" Goldschmidt denounced him as "a traitor", "a liar" and the man responsible for the death of millions of British fish at the hands of the Spanish during the early years of the EC.

Grocer Misconduct

His voice rising to a mad crescendo, Sir Jimmy Goldfish accused the frail octogenarian of "pretending not to remember the incident.

"You haf betrayed your country and handed it over to ze enemy. Now you must pay the price — which is death by a million pamphlets."

It was difficult to imagine that the doddery white-haired old man described by neighbours as "a model citizen who sat at home playing his organ" had once commanded an elite squad of Toriz and had earned the nickname "Obergrosserführer" by his ruthless negotiations over Britain's signing of the Treaty of Rome.

Loonybore Heath

But after only a few minutes the jury walked out in disgust.

"He is a pathetic man," said the foreman, "but enough of Sir James Goldsmith. Anyway, it all happened a long time ago and I don't want to miss Emmerdale again."

It is estimated that the campaign to bring Grosserawitz to justice has cost Sir James £500 million.

How they are not related any more

Roger Moore · *Luisa Moore*

Old Moore	Miss Moneypenny
St Thomas Moore	Miss Manypounds
St Charles Moore	Miss Moneybags
The Saint	"Pursey" Galore
Roger Moore	Plenty O'Loote
Roger Someone Else	Tiffany Account
007½ (Million Pounds Poorer)	**007½ (Million Pounds Richer)**

"Hmm, it's all so tempting… Cassoulet, Jugged Hare, perhaps the venison… Oh, what the hell, I'll have the fish!"

6 MILLION TODDLERS ABUSED EVERY SECOND — IT'S OFFICIAL

by Our Bogus Statistics Staff **Enid Rancid**

AN official report published by the National Society For the Propaga-tion of Cooked-Up Statistics (NSPCS) reveals that the newspapers will print absolutely anything without bothering to check it, when it relates to toddlers or child abuse.

The report claims that there are "17 billion incidents of child abuse in Britain" every day, ranging from looking at a child while it is asleep in bed to talking about it behind its back.

As a result, billions of Britain's 15 million toddlers are growing in a "seriously traumatised state".

A radical solution is called for, says the report, involving:

● **the transfer of huge sums of money from taxpayers to the NSPCS**

● **all parents to be arrested**

● **all toddlers to be taken into care**

● **toddlers to be properly looked after in secure institutions under the expert care of highly trained paedophiles** (surely 'caring social workers'? Ed).

National Curriculum

(Module 94)
Morality Test

Name: Do not put name here as it cannot be revealed for legal reasons.

1. Do you know the difference between good and bad?
a) Yes
b) No.

2. Have you lied in the above question?
a) Yes
b) Mind your own business or I'll thump you.

3. Is it wrong to kill?
a) I didn't do it
b) I blame my parents
c) I blame society.

4. Why is selling cocaine wrong?
a) It isn't
b) Do you want some?
c) My mobile number is 0890 37242.

5. Look at these two knives. Which one is yours?
a) I threw it away
b) I always carry a gun
c) You're asking a lot of questions for someone who wants to stay alive.

6. Is it right for Mrs Shephard to force you to take this examination in order to help Mr Major win the election?
a) Who is Mrs Shephard?
b) Who is Mr Major?
c) What is an election?

Time allowed: 3 years (12 months suspended)

Teach Yourself Latin Partem XCIV

Remembering what you learnt last week, translate the following sentences into English:

1. Conradus Niger divissimus Canadiensis est.

2. Barbara Amiella puella pulcherrima est.

3. Niger amat Barbaram et conjugat illam.

4. Redactor Telegraphi, Carolus Plus Etoniensis, donet columnam ad Barbaram.

5. Columnus Barbarae tediusissimus est.

6. Circulatio Telegraphi descendit celerrime.

7. Murdochus in America ridet.

Pre-School Nursery Facility Rhymes

Georgie Porgie, pudding and pie,
Kissed the girls and made them cry.
When the boys came out to play,
Georgie Porgie was accused of sexual
harassment and creating a hostile
offensive environment and after a
summary tribunal he
was taken away.

CRISIS IN SCHOOLS

And who is the Prime Minister?

Er… Oasis

I think that's enough about Johnny Bryan

MP CONFESSES TO SECRET 'LOVE TALKS'

by Our Political Staff
Jerry Gayes

THE senior Liberal MP Mr Paddy Pantsdown admitted last night that he had had secret meetings with an attractive young leader of the Labour Party, Mr Tony Blair.

"We met several times," confessed Pollsdown, "but nothing improper took place."

However, letters that have come into Private Eye's possession (because we bought them) reveal that an intense affair developed between the two men. In one passionate missive Mr Ashtray declared:

Dear Tony,
We have so much in common. We must be together more. Perhaps forever. We have so much to share, you and I, and we could make a go of it for certain. I know that you are worried about your party finding out and I too have that problem. But we must be brave and follow the love that dare not speak its name, ie a Lib/Lab Pact.
Yours sincerely,
The Rt Hon Patrick Passionfruit,
The Old Cottage, Yeovil.

A Doctor writes

Gulf War Syndrome

AS A Doctor, I am often told: "There is no such thing as Gulf War Syndrome."

Recently, however, new research has indicated that the Gulf War has produced alarming effects in Conservative Cabinet Ministers.

Symptoms include long periods of smugness, later followed by profound sweating and panic attacks. The victim may feel extremely uncomfortable, hot under the collar and deeply anxious about being revealed as an appalling liar.

Technically known as *Soamensis uturnus normalis*, the Gulf Syndrome is so called because of the enormous gulf between the Minister's initial remarks and the truth which emerges later.

If you are worried about Nicholas Soames, then you should not be concerned. This is very common indeed.

© A. Doctor.

COURT CIRCULAR

KLOSTERS, TUESDAY

HIS Royal Highness the Prince of Wales will arrive today at the bottom of the Ingmarberg Run accompanied by His Royal Highness the Prince Harry. They will be greeted by a Reception Committee led by Signor Slizi Papparazzo from Oggi magazine, Mr Ron Guzzer of the Sun newspaper and Señor Zumi Lenzi of the Spanish periodical Ola! After the photo-call, HRH will address the Committee on the importance of them pissing off pretty pronto while he gets on with his skiing holiday.

The Procession of the Ski Lifts will be formed as follows:

First Ski Lift
HRH the Prince of Wales, Miss Tara Masalata-Tomkinson, the Duke of Klosters.

Second Ski Lift
Chief Instructor Otto von Zippentrouser, HRH the Prince Harry of Ludgrove, Miss Tigella ("Tiggy") Winkel-Wankel.

Third Ski Lift
Miss Tiramisu Huntley-Palmer, Miss Santa Klaus von Bulow, Inspector Quentin Palmer-Tomkinson of the Royal Windsor Constabulary (Ski Division).

First Helicopter
M. Jean-Paul Snooper of Paris Match, Sven Snatchesson of the Stockholm photo-journal Skøp and Lady Antonia Holden of the Daily Express.

Hiding In Chalet
Mrs Smythe-Smith (HRH Camilla Palmer-Bowles).

Man In Chalet Garden Disguised As Snowman
Mr Eddie Bogg of the News of the World.

"We're going home soon – go and nick a car"

Channel 4 – Secret Lives

Douglas Bastard – The Truth

BEHIND the façade of a neurotic, whingeing self-pitying disabled misfit the courageous Secret Lives team reveal that Bastard was also a Battle of Britain pilot and national hero who helped to win the war. Amazingly, Bastard was not his real name — he was originally called 'Bader'.

NEXT WEEK: Jesus. The Secret Lives team discover that far from being the meek and mild character of Christian propaganda, Jesus was a difficult, abrasive troublemaker who:

● *Had a difficult relationship with his mother.*

● *Was hated by many of those he worked with, including star witness J. Iscariot.* (That's enough Channel 4. Ed)

TOP SECRET

FOR YOUR EYES ONLY, MR BOND

Sir James and the Marmite Soldiers on manoeuvres in Brighton

So, Mr Major-Bond. At last you have seen the reality of my Marmite Army at my Brighton Rally.

Impressive, nicht wahr? Frightening, almost.

And now, after our little show of strength, it is but just one more tiny step and the moment when I assume supreme power will have arrived!

And so, Mr Major, you are wondering, like the whole nation, what the first Goldsmith administration will look like.

(Strokes white cricket jumper, formerly the property of Mr G. Borecott, Yorkshire and England)

Carla, the seating plan for my Cabinet...

(Enter sultry temptress in diamante cheetah-skin leotard, the gift of Chief Brutalezi, First Minister and Life President of the Kingdom of Zululalia. She presses button to activate 80-foot-high telescreens showing secret Cabinet Room in the bowels of Fishpaste Towers)

Let me introduce them, one by one. I think you will find some faces you recognise.

Firstly, my Deputy and Minister For Population Control, Mr John Aspinall, and his team of highly trained man-eating tigers.

Next, my Minister of Finance, my old friend Mr Jim Slater. No one has a greater grasp of money than he does.

Now, a most important portfolio — Minister for Information and Propaganda, Mr Cokeupthenos, owner of the only Greek column nobody wants.

My Home Secretary and Minister for Morality, Mr Paul Johnson, owner of a large number of English columns which nobody wants.

And this brings me neatly on to my Minister for Fish, Dr Christopher Barkworth of the Sunday Telegraph.

(Strange bespectacled figure appears, dragging small son with "Vote Sir Jams" badge on)

Leader of the House of Lords, Lord Lucan, declared innocent by my Lord Chancellor, Lord Carter-Ruck of the Ritz.

Now, Mr Bond, wake up. You will be wondering about the constitutional position.

I am sure you would agree that our so-called Royal Family, like our politicians, have — how shall I put it? — failed the nation. That is why they must be flushed down the toilet. Instead the people of Britain must be given a monarch they can look up to.

May I present His Majesty King Edward the Fox!

(Mad figure in plus-fours comes on, accompanied by massed choirs singing Vivat Rex)

THE KING: I say! Jolly good show, Jimmy! Got rid of all those pinkoes and Bertie Woofters.

So, Mr Major-Bond. Your little game is almost up. Your brief moment of fame is almost at an end, before you are swept down the toilet of history.

And then begins the glorious new era of Referendumism, which will last for a thousand years.

(The leader climbs into nuclear-powered straitjacket and takes off to the nearest Black Hole to address huge rally of anti-protons and quarks)

Issued on behalf of the Referendum Party of Great Britain

"And is this antagonistic relationship with your father an ongoing thing?"

YOU BIG GIRL'S BLOUSE

THE ALTERNATIVE ROCKY HORROR SERVICE BOOK

No. 94: A Service Of Thanksgiving To Almighty God For His Precious Gift Of Homosexuality (to be held in Southwark Cathedral by kind permission of the Rt Rev Cedric de Gayetrouser, Bishop of Southwark)

The President: Hullo.

All: Well, hullo.

The President: You may now give each other a Sign of Peace.

(All embrace their partners)

President: We shall now sing our first hymn, "Gay's My Soul, The King of Heaven".

INTERCESSIONS

President: Brothers and sisters, we are gathered here together to thank God for our sexual orientation.

All: We thank thee.

President: For the joy of moustaches, earrings and leather trousers.

All: We thank thee.

President: For the joy of cruising, cottaging and not to have the total nightmare of family life.

All: We thank thee.

(There shall here be a sermon given by a lesbian priestess)

Brothers and sisters. Aren't men awful? Except gay men, of course. They are great. But the one thing that really gets me going is the total homophobic intolerance of the Church throughout the ages, which has burnt gay men and women at the stake. And make no mistake, there are still loads of self-styled Christians today who would do the same again if they had the chance. And now let us celebrate our total hatred of homophobia by singing a hymn which has been specially written for this historic service.

HYMM

All things gay and beautiful
All creatures gay and small
All things gay and wonderful
Homophobes — we hate them all.

President: Go forth and do not multiply.

All: Amen.

BRITISH STREETS TO CHARGE ADMISSION

by Our Heritage Staff
Victoria and Albert Museum

THE Heritage Secretary, Mrs Virginia Bottomley, today announced that from next Sunday it would be necessary to charge an entrance fee for all Britain's streets.

Opponents of the scheme claimed that the British public already owns the streets and furthermore pays substantial taxes for their upkeep. But Mrs Bottomley rejected these arguments as "dated, out-moded and completely right".

She continued: "People who want to use our streets should have to pay. The streets may be part of our nation's heritage, but they are very expensive to maintain and the money raised from admission charges could be used to fund more important projects such as share option schemes for directors of privatised utilities."

The British Museum is 238 years old.

"Before you jump, could you tell us where the tin-opener is?"

School news

St Cakes

Pride Term (formerly Lent) begins today. There are 375 boys and 385 girls in the school. E. John (Cross-dressers) is Head Boy and Head Girl. Miss J. Winterton (Burchills) is Captain of Le Creuset. The speaker on St Cakes Day (June 2nd) will be the MP for Harlow, Mr Jerry Hayes (OC), and there will be a concert by the school orchestra immediately afterwards. They will play work by Sir Michael Tippett, Lord Britten, and Sir Frederick Mercury. There will be a performance by the choir of the St Matthew Paris on March 14th. Outings will be held on St Tatchell's Day (March 31st). The Gay OC Lodge will meet at the LeatherZone, Old Compton Street, London W1. Tickets from the Secretary John Lyttle (OC), c/o The Independent.

History For Schools
(as featured in the National Curriculum)

The 94th Crusade

IN THE last years before the Millennium, the forces of Islam were on the march across the globe. Nation after nation succumbed to the followers of the Prophet. In far-away Afghanistan, the mighty Taliban held sway, and in Algeria, Morocco, Palestine, France, and a host of other kingdoms there too the standard of Allah was raised high.

But in fair England a wise Prince did live, whose name was Charles the Woolly. And he was known throughout the land of Albion as a bit of an idiot *(shurely 'a scholar and wise man'? Ed)*.

And Charles was titled the Defender of the Faith, so when he heard of the march of Islam he called together his counsellors and said: "I have had a vision."

And they groaned and said: "Not another one."

And Charles told them: "It is high time that we in the west responded to the challenge of Islam."

And the counsellors were pleased and asked: "Does this mean war?"

"No," said the Prince. "I think Islam has a lot to teach us. They have a spiritual awareness that we in the west have sadly lost. I mean, our churches are just hopeless, aren't they? When you think about it, these mosques are just terrific. The Muslim chaps have this sense of oneness which keeps them very much in touch with the sort of thingie…"

And the counsellors buried their heads in despair.

NEXT EPISODE: How King Charles the Woolly became King Suleiman-ben-Rushdie the Woolly.

BLONDE WOMAN IN LOVE SPLIT SHOCK WITH MAN

by Our International News Staff **Phil Space**

A BLONDE woman has today sensationally either split up from the man she married or got back together with him. Or neither.

The happy or unhappy couple were last night seen leaving a smart restaurant together or separately or with some other people.

Friends of the couple said: "It doesn't surprise us at all. We knew that they were having problems or that they were always made for each other, whichever it is."

The couple called Pammy and Tommy or Mick and Jerry or Sherry and Gazza, or something similar have agreed to consult lawyers or marriage guidance counsellors or newspapers as they try to save or destroy their marriage.

The man has sworn that he will give up drink, drugs and other women or that he won't. The blonde woman has accepted this or finally had enough of him and chucked him out, so *(continued in all newspapers ad nauseam)*

27

She Needs Your Help

AS Christmas approaches and the season of goodwill descends on us once more, let us all spare a thought for those less fortunate than ourselves.

Fergie is an unemployed mother of two who at the age of 37 is destitute. She is £4 million in debt, through no fault of yours, and she has tried everything to get some form of income without having to do anything. Hers is a pitiful tale.

She has sucked men's toes, written bad books, appeared in *Hello!* magazine and advertised cameras on American television. She has even been reduced to borrowing children's stories and trying to sell them.

Please, please, please give generously to Fergie this Christmas. Without your help she will end up as a Royal centrefold in *Playboy*. Spare her and yourself this.

Send to: FERGIE IN NEED, Box 7394, Dallas.

Rudolph the Brown-Nose Reindeer

Give your friends a nasty shock!!

WILL SELF Horror Mask

Hours of fun with this lifelike latex mask of Britain's most famous novelist, restaurant critic and drug addict!

Watch the kiddies scream with terror as they think that Will Self has walked into the room.

Price: 2p for 4 masks

To Be Used In Schools

New Carols For Christmas From The Prince Charles Multi-Faith Songbook

Good King Suleiman looked out
On the feast of Ramadan,
When the sand lay all about,
Deep and crisp like the Taliban
Brightly shone the crescent moon that night
Though the frost was cruel,
When a poor man came in sight
Gathering winter fuel.

"Hither, wife, and stand four paces behind me,
If thou knows it telling,
Yonder fuel-stealer who is he?
Where and what his dwelling?"
"Sire, he lives a good league hence
Underneath the Mosque,
He deserves a hundred lashes and
His hand cut off."

PLUS

★ *Away in a Mecca*
★ *O little town of Islamabad*
★ *Unto us a son is born says Imran Khan*
★ *Silent Night because all the carols have been banned*

ROBERT THOMPSON

"Nuk! Don't spit at people, it's not nice"

Those Carey/ Pope John-Paul discussions in full

Carey: Greetings, Your Holiness.

Pope: Buon giorno, Signor Inglese.

Carey: Our hope is that our two great churches can move into ever closer union.

Pope: Super corpus meum, amicus. Detestemus ordinationem feminarum.

Carey: I think, er, in these times of moral uncertainty…

Pope: Abominatione, sodomistici et lesbiani in duomo santo di Southwark *(spits on floor)*. Tutti frutti.

Carey: Thank you very much, Your Holiness, for these reassurances. We go forward together.

ANSWERS TO THE CHRISTMAS QUIZ

(Continued from page 94)

(Continued from page 94)

3. A rusbridger is a Belgian term meaning a ratcatcher (from the original Walloon *Rütz* = rat and *Brudger* = a man with a bag).

4. The odd one out is Mohamed al-Fayed. All the others hold British passports.

5. If Mr Snodgrass left home at 8.15 a.m. and walked at a maximum speed of 4.3 km/hr he would arrive at Waterloo before the 7.15 a.m. train from Bristol Parkway. He could therefore not have murdered Mrs Marsh in the Vicarage.

6. Princess Diana, the Duchess of York, Paula Yates, Moll Flanders.

7. Pamela Anderson and Peter Mandelson.

8. Alan Sked, Sir James Goldsmith, Screaming Lord Sutch. They all got two votes.

9. Humphrey Lyttleton, Humphrey Bogart, John Humphrys, Humphrey the Cat.

TERRY CHRISTMAS!

I've got myself a couple of lovely birds

29

UPFRONTERS

goes to the most glamorous New Year parties in town

"**L-l-am** a bad boy," says the Oasis star as the **Chase** for **Lorraine** is on!?!? From now on, it's "What's the Story, Luton Airport?"?!?! We reckon she's his new **Gal-lagher**?!?!

Here's a **Lumley** lady!?! And look who Ab-Fab's **Joanna** is partying with?! None other than the Independent's top columnist **Suzanne Moore**!?! The Moore the merrier, sweetie darling?!? Independent ladies indeed!?!

"Ooh-aah, **Juliaah**!! **Cantonot** she score with **Eric**?!? If she wants to get United with her French fancy maybe she should try the full strip!?! Or perhaps an early bath together?!? **Carling**, you were wonderful!?!!

Don't cry Crocodile Shoes for me **Jimmy Nail**?!! That's what **Madonna** must be singing?! The two stars of the hit movie *Evita* make a lovely Per-on!?! Have you Eva seen anything like it?!?

He's not over the **Hill** yet!? Watch out, **Emma**, he's a real **Damon** with the ladies and he's not a-**Freud** to show it!?! Care for a spin?! Or is he just a bit too fast for a presenter-ble girl like you?!? Vrrm! Vrrm!!

Who's collared Ms **Mirren**?! Don't worry, **Helen**, it's just **William**!?! The Times might be a-changin' but **Rees-Mogg** is always a gentleman!? He's still in his *Prime* and I *Suspect* you're fascinated by his views on the Single European Currency!?!

(That's enough pisspoor captions to dreary PR photos. Ed)

RECORD FIGURES FOR TV'S DUL BOY

by Spectator TV Staff **James Delboyingpole**

THE inexplicably long-running TV character Dul Boy broke all records this Christmas when an extraordinary 0 million people watched him appear for the last time.

The adventures of Dul Boy in the series *Only Fools and Arses* has proved one of the least popular sitcoms of all time and has made the ambitious loser from two rooms in Brixton a nationwide figure of fun.

Plonker

But this Christmas Dul Boy, otherwise known as John Major, is finally quitting.

There will be no more hilarious escapades with Dul Boy and his dodgy friends trying to flog off the nation's assets at rock bottom prices.

Luvvley Jobless

Never again will we see him narrowly avoiding the law as he tries to set up just one more deal.

Even his creator, Margaret Thatcher, says: "The nation has had enough of him. He was quite funny at first but now he's just boring. I'm working on a new character called Costa Del Boy played by Michael Portillo."

John Major is 22 million votes behind.

PETER McLIE

THE COLUMN THAT GETS THE SACK FROM PUNCH

THERE is a new trend amongst the young folk, I hear. With the coming of the New Year they decide to turn over a new leaf and make changes to their lives. Some take up smoking, others decide to put on weight. My own idea is to get a job. I have a feeling that this will become a huge fashion in all classes of our society. I even have a name for these decisions — "New Year Trouser Presses".

DID YOU read the story about Fergie in yesterday's Sunday Mirror? Maybe there wasn't one. Who knows? But if there had been, I wonder what it would have said? "Fergie and the Trouser Press" — that would have been a good headline.

WHAT did you get for Christmas? I had a number of goodies in my stocking, including a bottle or two of a strange purple whisky called "Meths".

But one gift baffled me completely — a large electrical device like an upright ironing board with a picture of a pair of trousers on it. Can anyone help, I wonder?

(You're Fayed. Ed.)

"I don't know, office parties just haven't been the same since I started working from home"

★ BEIJING TIMES

'Better Dead Than Read'

I Deng

GREAT WORLD LEADER DEAD

Tribute Flows In

THE people of Britain were in mourning today for the god-like figure they called "The Father of His People".

He was the last of the great world statesmen who emerged in the years after World War Two.

Glo-sah Heath, affectionately known as "Dung", lived through turbulent times, and fell out of favour during the Non-Cultural Revolution, when Britain was ruled by the mad dictator Mao-Tse-Thatch.

No Mourning Crowd

In his later years, Heath was best known for his unshakeable support for the Chinese leadership.

He spoke out courageously in defence of all their policies, most notably the shooting of students in Tiananmen Square, the torture and massacring of Tibetan monks and the regular sending of large cheques to himself.

On Other Pages

Why Did Heath Never Mate? *asks top Panda*	14
Your Bicycles Tonight	18
Unfunny Cartoon by Wok	23

Who are they — the front-runners for China's Top Hot Seat

1 Hu Hee, 78, currently First Secretary of the Party Praesidium and adopted heir of the late Hu Yu. At 84, he is considered to be a reformist moderate who believes in maintaining the Party's absolute control over all aspects of Chinese life. His son No Wun is head of the China-Hong Kong Venture Socialist Banking Co.

2 Hang Em Hi, 92, currently Chairman of the People's Forum For A New China. At 96, Hang is a moderate reformist who believes in suppressing all forms of dissent. His son Gih Me Sum runs the China-Hong Kong People's Finance and Car Rental Corporation.

3 Sen Din Tank, 104, currently head of the People's Liberation Army Gulag Division. At 108, Sen is seen as a conservative with hard-line moderate tendencies, who believes that nearly everyone in the country should be arrested to ensure stability. His Son Chee Poh runs the fashionable People's Lucky Dragon Disco and Karaoke Bar in downtown Shanghai.

4 Lon Gon, 128, currently dead though still revered as a veteran of the Long March. Lon, 178, believed strongly in the values of Marxist-Leninist-Maoism and the Four Great Principles, namely Arrest Them, Torture Them, Shoot Them and Keep All The Money. His son died in mysterious circumstances during the Cultural Revolution after describing Mao Tse-Tung as only "the greatest man who ever lived".

5 Sweet and Sour Pork Balls with Crispy Noddles and Special Fried Rice for Two. *(That's enough front-runners. Ed.)*

PARENTS MUST BE IN BED BY 10PM SAYS NEW LABOUR

by Our Home Affairs Correspondent **Nanny State**

MR DAVID Blunkett today unveiled his 10-Point Plan for Better Parenting, to be made compulsory within five minutes of his New Labour government storming to power.

1. All children must be given half an hour's reading aloud of traditional fairy tales and nursery rhymes every night.

2. All children must be in bed no later than 7.30pm, having brushed their teeth, put their toys away tidily, folded their clothes neatly, said their prayers, gone to the toilet and written a thank-you letter to granny for her postal order not less than one side of A4 in length with no spelling mistakes.

3. Children are not permitted to watch more than half-an-hour's television a day and then only in the following categories: wild life films, animated versions of Old Testament or classical stories, Dad's Army or repeats of the Muppet Show.

4. Children must not be naughty at any time, otherwise the terrible Mr Prescott will come round and spank them on their bottoms but only in a caring manner.

5. Er…

6. That's it.

"I accept that he goes with prostitutes. I just wish he wasn't so blatant about it"

DENG: A NATION MOURNS

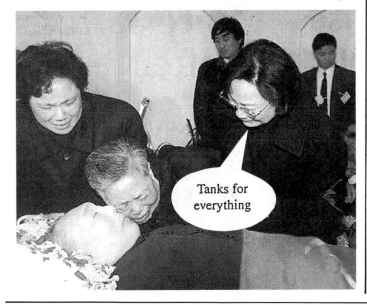

Tanks for everything

BBC Reith Lectures In Full

This year's Reith lectures are given by Dr Deirdre Z. Spartenburger, Professor of Racism Awareness Studies at the University of Malcolm X, New Dworkin.

THE underlying quandary epitomised in any multi-culturalised analysis of the implicitness of "us-ness" and "them-ness" as imposed by any dominant hierarchist paradigm on the thought-patterns of a de-socialised and therefore explicitly alienated sub-grouping, which defies universalist norms and yet, paradoxically, conforms to those very acculturalised ethic systems *(continues in this vein for several hours before telling highly improbable anecdote about her adoptive four year old son)*. "On his very first day in high school he was asked to watch a 'colour' television set. But he had been so brainwashed by the white liberal establishment to pretend that 'colour' was not important, that he burst into tears and told the teachers that he couldn't see the television because he was in a state of culturated de-racinated ethnic trauma syndrome." *(Continues anecdote for several more hours)*.

The Truth about Tough Street Talk

Tough Street Talk

Translation

Traditional Nursery Rhymes No. 94

Baa Baa clone sheep
Have you any wool?
Yes sir
Yes sir
Yes sir
Yes sir
Yes sir
(continued page 94)

Lookalikes

Ena Sharples   **William Hague**

Sir,

I wonder if any other readers have noticed the striking resemblance between the secretary of state for Wales and the late Ena Sharples? Are they by any chance related? I think we should be told.

Yours faithfully,
A.A. LOVELACE,
Hatfield, Herts.

Elton   **Wallace**

Sir,

Pawing over the EVENING POST recently whose face should I see grinning out at me but that of my loving master Wallace sporting a ridiculous wig! What a relief when I later realised it was only Elton John — certainly a close shave there!

GROMIT,
Heaton Mersey, Stockport.

Cartland   **Winner**

Sir,

Has anyone else noticed the remarkable resemblance between the well-known novelist and the large food critic? They say that there is a link between romance and food, but I think there is a winner here. I think we should be told.

Yours faithfully,
ANTHONY WEAVER,
Malta.

Charlton   **Picasso**

Sir,

Am I right in thinking that the popular footballer Bobby Charlton had another brother, who, having failed to make the grade as a footballer, ran away to Spain and became some sort of artist? Perhaps your readers could throw some more light on this matter?

With compliments,
ENA B. HIGNETT,
Edinburgh.

Maxwell   **Snowman**

Sir,

I imagine, given your justifiable preoccupation with the old fraud, you will have noticed that Robert Maxwell is staging a bid for rehabilitation disguised as a snowman on the front of the new edition of the RADIO TIMES.

I am sure that you will not let him get away with it!

Yours faithfully,
MIKE KAY,
Via e-mail.

Dawes   **Horlick**

Sir,

Surely I am not the only person to notice the startling resemblance between high-flying mother-of-five Nicola Horlick and the baby-faced scoremaster on BBC2's Shooting Stars, George Dawes. Are they, perchance, related in some way? I think Vic, Bob, Mark and Ulrik-ka-ka-ka-ka should be told.

Yours faithfully,
TIM MASTERS,
Via e-mail.

Fergie   **Debbi**

Sir,

Have any other readers noticed the similarity between the new whacko Mrs M. Jackson and the Duchess of York? Could this be the way to clear debts?

Regards,
HAMISH WARBURTON,
Steyning, W. Sussex.

Mme Cézanne   **Mandelson**

Sir,

Has anyone noticed the remarkable resemblance between Cézanne's wife in the painting "Madame Cézanne in a Yellow Armchair" and the legendary "spin doctor" Peter Mandelson? I wonder if they could possibly be related in some way?

Yours faithfully,
JONATHAN FARRELL,
London N7.

McCartney   **McAliskey**

Sir,

Looking at a recent photograph of Bernadette McAliskey talking to reporters, I noticed a striking resemblance between her and our recently knighted Beatle, Paul McCartney. But whereas one has recently been a visitor to Buckingham Palace, the other has recently visited Holloway. There can have been very little similarity between Her Majesty's Prison and Her Majesty's Residence!

Yours,
MISS MULLICENT KINTYRE,
"D" Wing, Orkney Open Prison, Scotland.

Schwarzenegger **Bottomley**

Sir,

Surely there can be no doubt, on closer examination of these pictures, of the relationship between those two "tough cookies" Arnold Schwarzenegger and Virginia Bottomley.

One can only surmise, however, that after the next General Election Mrs Bottomley won't "be back" and her political career is "terminated".

MRS ENID B. CONAN,

Oxon.

Ravanelli **Les Amants**

Sir,

If, as anticipated, Middlesborough's expensive Italian import Fabrizio Ravanelli leaves the club, a suggested replacement could be the model for Magritte's "Les Amants", as they both share a remarkable similarity.

Yours sincerely,
ALLAN GODFREY,

Knebworth.

Goldsmith **Flea**

Sir,

I was very struck by this resemblance between The Ghost of a Flea by William Blake and Sir James Goldsmith. Is there a relationship between Blake's vision and Putney's visionary? But I think I'd rather not be told.

Cheers,
VANILLA BEER,

London SE18.

Thatcher **Evans**

Sir,

I wonder if any other readers have noticed the remarkable resemblance between the "new look" Lady Thatcher and the Young Persons' Popular Entertainer Mr Chris Evans? Could it be that another senior female political figure will be happily reunited with a long-lost love-child? Though perhaps Mr David Evans MP (no relation?) would prefer a more robust description.

Yours faithfully,
NICK READ,
Cromford, Derbyshire.

Bushell **Themistocles**

Sir,

I wonder if any of your readers have noticed the startling resemblance between the noble but hairy Garry Bushell, "renaissance man", and heavyweight SUN columnist, and the equally hirsute Themistocles, Athenian politician and architect of the glorious Greek victory at Salamis in 480 BC?

Does Mr Bushell have any Greek in him? His telly reviews owe so much to classical civilisation.

Yours faithfully,
PHILIP FREEMAN,
Pinner, Middlesex.

Rory **Roarer**

Sir,

Now that Jerry Hayes's boyish good looks have suddenly graced the nation's front pages, I couldn't help noticing his resemblance to Rory McGrath, the less well known British Telecom employee. What different lives they both must lead. I wonder if they are related?

Yours,
ENA B. HOSKINS,
Barking Job Centre.

Punch **Gambaccini**

Sir,

There is a remarkable similarity between the former dole collector Mr Punch and the job seeker Paul Gambaccini. Could they be related?

L. WIRTZ,
London NW10.

Blair **Imp**

Sir,

On a recent visit to Lincoln Cathedral I was struck by the pronounced resemblance of the Lincoln Imp to the leader of the HM Opposition, the Hon. Tony Blair.

On further investigation I discovered that the Imp, an impudent young disciple of the Devil, had climbed on the altar, laughing with derision, and threatened to throw out the Bishop, the Dean, the organist and most of the congregation, before he was stopped by divine intervention. How very different from New Labour.

Yours sincerely,
CHRIS JACKSON,

Lincoln.

Charles **Lebed**

Sir,

Perusing my Sunday papers, I wonder if I am the only person to notice a distinctly worrying resemblance between General Alexander Lebed and Craig Charles in panto gear.

I think we — and the Russian people — should be told.

Yours,
CHARLIE HARRIS,
London NW3.

Daily Mail

GOOSEPAPER OF THE YEAR 35p

HATTERSLEY KILLER DOG IN LABOUR ROYAL MURDER

by Our Man In The Park
RAY GOSLING

THERE WAS no mistaking the look of sheer terror on the face of innocent cuddly toddler Goose B (whose name cannot be revealed for legal reasons) as the bloodthirsty former Labour Deputy Leader released his homicidal Rottweiler, Jaws, in St James Royal Park last week.

Seconds later the innocent gosling was a mass of bloody feathers while the dog's owner chuckled and gave him a chocolate chewy.

Make no mistake, this is what lies in store for Britain when Labour *(cont. p. 94)*

(cont. p. 94)

ON OTHER PAGES: Vote Conservative

TV HIGHLIGHTS

Identical Twins
Channel 4

ALAN AND Kenneth Clark were separated at birth. One was brought up in a castle, the other sent to a state school. Uncannily, both became senior figures in the Conservative party. Though one is left of centre and the other extremely right of centre, they both share a deep respect for one another's viewpoint. Alan believes Kenneth is "a vulgar little parvenu who probably buys his own shoes". Kenneth thinks Alan is a "lazy, good-for-nothing aristocrat who landed us in the shit over Iraq".

Tonight they are reunited in the television studio where they exhibit an almost supernatural similarity in their ability to talk rubbish in the hope of getting elected.

A Taxi-Driver writes

Every week a well-known cabbie is asked to comment on an issue of topical importance.

This week: Hand-Gun Legislation by **Monty Mirror** (Cab No. 732748)

Do you see those MPs who voted against banning the guns? What a bloody disgrace! Right in front of the mothers who lost their kids! Bastards! They can't have no feelings in their bodies can they? Honestly, I ask you. What kind of respect is that for the dead?

There's only one way to deal with people like that. Line 'em up against the wall and shoot 'em. It's the only language they understand. I 'ad that David Mellor in the back of the cab once. He gave me a CD. Nice bloke…

NEXT WEEK: **Reg Snozzer** *on why the Frogs are to blame for the Chunnel fire.*

BRILLO OF PAD GOES HOME

by Our Scottish Staff **Sharon Stone and Professor Norman Scone**

THE historic Brillo of Pad, long revered by the Scots as one of their most cherished relics was returned to Scotland yesterday amidst much rejoicing in England.

For over 10 years the Brillo has been embedded beneath the bottom of the so-called Dirty Digger and enshrined in Wapping.

Now at last, thanks to pressure by English campaigners, the Brillo is to be taken home with due ceremony to its native Edinburgh where it will be kept beneath the bottom of the Barclay Brothers.

The Brillo will be on show at the headquarters of the Scotsman Newspaper between 9am and 5pm (Mon to Sunday).

According to the ancient poem by Scottish Bard William Rees-McGonnagal:

Scotland can nae be truly glad
Till the homecoming of yon
Brillo of Pad.

The Brillo of Pad is 47.

BIRT UNVEILS NEW-LOOK BBC NEWS

by Our Media Staff **Phil Space**

MR JOHN Birt, the director-general of the BBC, yesterday announced another huge shake-up of the Corporation's news output, following the one he announced last week.

In response to a £250 million marketing survey, conducted with the aid of 7,500 "focus groups" in 12 sub-regions of the country, Mr Birt said: "BBC News has become a minority enclave of middle-aged, middle-class, white attitudes which no longer represent the views of more than 90 per cent of our audience.

"What the BBC must do is to appeal to a much younger audience, particularly those who are not interested in news."

What You Will See In The New-Look BBC News

● *Bong!*

Chris Evans (for it is he): Hi kids.

● *Bong!*

Evans: This is the news, OK? Telling it like it is.

● *Bong!*

Evans: Right. Honk if you're watching. Bonk if you're not.

● *Bonk!*

Evans: And now... the Spice Girls.

(There follows a video of certain female young persons cavorting to the sound of raucous music)

Evans: Great. And now the weather, right? Over to Gazza in the weather studio.

(Man with dyed blond hair is discovered seated drunk in a dentist's chair)

Gazza: Burp!

Evans: Great. And now some late news. I want more money or I'm not doing this any more.

Continuity: And now on BBC-1, *Panorama* looks at the new Spice Girls video. And later on *Newsnight,* Jeremy Paxman interviews Patsy Kensit...

Branarg's Hamlet
Cast in full (3rd hour)

Hamlet, Prince of Denmark	Kenneth Branarg
Ghost's Father	Woody Allen
Osric's Brother	Arnold Schwarzenegger
Yorick's Mother-in-Law	Ruby Wax
Rosencrantz's Niece	Michelle Pfeiffer
Yorick's Dog	Lassie
2nd Ghost's Sister-in-Law	Roseanne Barr
Fortinbras' Hairdresser	O.J. Simpson
Gravediggers' Agent	Danny De Vito
Ophelia's Psychotherapist	Frasier (from *Frasier*)
People in Danish Hostelry	Cast of Cheers

(continued Hour 94)

Peggy Ashcroft's Lovers In Full

(continued from page one) Sir Herbert Beerbohm-Tree; Mahatma Gandhi; Lytton Strachey; Laurel and Hardy; Gilbert and George; Gilbert and Sullivan; Take That; Sir Peregrine Worsthorne; Cecil Rhodes; Michael Foot; Sir John Gielguid; Sir Ian McKellen; Sir Kenneth Branagh; Terry Thomas; Damien Hirst; Sir John Harvey-Jones; W.G. Grace. *(That's enough lovers. Ed. No it's not. The Late Dame Peggy)*

END OF LINE SALE
EVERYTHING MUST GO — EXCEPT THE TRAINS

(UNDERSOLD) *(UNDERSOLD)*

Due to a forthcoming general election and the need to raise funds at any price, there now arises a once-in-a-lifetime opportunity to buy an underground network — complete or in parts — for your very own.

It consists of the following items:

● **100,000 miles of track and tunnel. Yours for £35 ono.**

● *100 trains decorated with world-renowned graffiti by local artists. £7.35 each.*

● **300 platforms complete with angry people wondering where the train is. £5 each or buy two and get one free.**

● *30 important mosaic murals by artist Sir Eduardo Paolozzarubbish. 10p each.*

● **35,000 escalators and lifts — some working. £1.50 (+ VAT).**

● *Tape recording of 1930s man saying "Mind The Gap", "Stand Clear of the Doors" and "Pass Right Down Inside the Cars". £1,783.24p.*

PLUS FREE!

● **200 assorted musicians, including guitarist singing Beatles selection, saxophonist playing Dave Brubeck's "Take Five", and African drummer playing medley of Zairean tribal hits.**

☞ Apply at once to Sir George Young, Minister of Transport quoting "Everything Must Go" offer.

The next privatisation will be along in 10 minutes. Customers are advised to use their cars.

GERMANY COMPLETELY WASHED UP

Yesterday in Bonn

by Our Political Staff **Frank Furt and Sir Isaiah Berlin**

A ONCE-proud nation, the economic miracle of Europe, now lies in ruins, writes our man at Wapping taking dictation from Conservative Central Office.

From Munich to Dusseldorf, from Stuttgart to Helsinki *(Get a map. Ed.)* the story is the same.

Starving toddlers roam the autobahns pitifully begging for scraps of apple strudel and liverwurst from the Turkish immigrants.

Giant rats escaping from the sewers devour the unburied corpses of the unemployed as pensioners wheel barrowloads of worthless deutschmarks to the empty sausage shops.

The once-great Bundesbank is now a dosshouse.

Yes, make no mistake, Herr Kohl's Germany is Alles Über or, to put it in plain English, All Over.

The German man in the strasse now looks with hungry eye towards Britain's Economic Miracle where our flourishing industries are the envy of the world.

Said one businessman, Herr Hans Madeupname: "If only we had a Prime Minister like your John Major I would not have to eat my children and sell my wife into prostitution to stay alive."

Hogarth's 300th Anniversary

H OGARTH's famous *Rake's Progress* (1997) is now on display in the House of Commons. *The Rake's Progress or Vice Rewarded* charts the rise and rise of one Alan Clarkwell in a series of narrative comic episodes. The sequence tells an instructive story about the perils of a life spent in drunkenness, philandering and politics. There aren't any.

In panel 3 (shown above) the high-living heir to a fortune Clarkwell seduces the wife *and* both daughters of a well-known judge which inevitably leads to no downfall at all. The Rake instead proceeds to make another fortune writing up his debauchery in his diaries. His subsequent appearance in the dock over arms sales does not dent his career either and in the last touching scene Clarkwell descends into madness and is consigned to Bedlam (the name given by 20th Century Londoners to the House of Commons). He then continues just as before.

THE SUN

Bullshit ON THE BOX

SO, THEY are going to sack Linsey from the Street. I've got a message for the bosses at Granada. I'd like to get her in the sack!

☐ NOSTROMO? Nostromosexual more like it with all those foreigners poncing about. It's time for the BBC to clean up its act.

☐ EASTENDERS is supposed to be realistic. So how come all the blacks don't get arrested for nicking your videos? Mind you, that Sharma in the drycleaners is a cracker. I wouldn't mind a tumble in the dryer with her!

☐ DO YOU want to know who I fancy most in Brookside? Sharon or Lynne or the new one, Mandy? Answer: none of them. I want all of them at once! Corrr!

BRITAIN's top television critic returns with another in-depth look at the medium only in tomorrow's Sun.

"Hello, darling – what do you do for a living?"

THE PRAT IN THE HAT

By Spin Dr. Seuss

There's nothing to do on a cold winter's day
So what could turn up to drive boredom away?
When suddenly plop! there dropped on the mat,
Some wonderful snaps of the Prat in the Hat!

"Look at me! Look at me!"
Says the Prat in the Hat
"I'm on the front page
Mr Blair can't do that!"

"I'm a respected world statesman.
I'm a serious figure."
Said the Prat in the Hat
As we all had a snigger.

"I don't think it's funny."
Said the Prat up the Khyber
As everyone chortled
And vowed to vote Lyber.
(Shurely 'Conservative'? Spin-Doctor Seussless)

---

89 PER CENT OF PUBLIC VOTE FOR ABOLITION OF CARLTON

by Our Media Staff Michael Greenbacks

IN THE biggest phone-in poll ever held in the history of television, 20 million viewers voted last night for the immediate removal of Carlton Television from any further part in Britain's national life.

"The television firm should be replaced by a blank screen," said an astonishing 94 per cent of those polled, although 6 per cent declared themselves in favour of 24-hour repeats of Dad's Army and Dr who.

A supplementary question, "Do you think Michael Green a fit and proper person to be the supreme head of a TV company?" was answered in the negative by a staggering 105 per cent.

Claire Long To Rayner Over Us

The phone-in came after a four-hour-long debate which featured many distinguished commentators from all walks of life.

Among those who spoke up in favour of Carlton were Sir Melvyn Barg, who told viewers: "This is democracy in action — two million people screaming abuse at each other in a TV studio can't be wrong."

He was supported by Sir Jeremy Paxperson, who said: "It's very important for ITV to put on this sort of low-grade rubbish, so that I look terrific on BBC2."

James Whitaker's All-maniac

But other speakers were violently opposed to the idea that Carlton should survive into the 21st century.

Said Sir Robin Day, 108: "In the good old days I was the only person who was allowed to be rude on television. Now everyone is at it."

He was backed up by a senior government minister Sir Tom Sackmeoriquit, who shouted: "It is outrageous that a cheap, nasty and vulgar company like Carlton should have been given a franchise in the first place just because they were the highest bidder.

"Whichever government was responsible should be thoroughly ashamed of themselves and deserve to be booted out at the next election."

Your Guide To Topical Fish*

1. Guppy *(Darius Etoniensis Fraudulosis)* DANGEROUS fish which benefits from incarceration away from other fish. If allowed free will poison environment. Thought to be extinct until recent reappearance.

2. Sir James Goldfish *(Marmitus Litigus Rex)* LARGE shark-like predator found on the Coast of Mexico. Tries to make other fish follow him out of the tank to their death.

3. Michael *(Legoverus Meteorologicus)* HARMLESS-looking specimen with moustache and glasses but can prove slippery when it leaves its mate and swims off with bird.

4. Wanda UNAMUSING fish which *(cont. p.94)*

*© P. Cook

"Hello... This is the Police. If you are being attacked from behind by a mad axe-murderer, press 'One' ..."

GNOMEBY'S

GRAND SALE of ROYAL MEMORABILIA relating to His Royal Highness the Duke of Windsor

Formerly the property of an Egyptian Gentleman (A. Fayed)

11.00 a.m.

Lot 1. Gold-plated Waterman's fountain pen, believed to be that used to sign the formal declaration of Abdication. Complete with maker's trademark and date of manufacture (1943). Plus two nibs (slightly bent, like owner). *Estimate: £27,000.*

Lot 2. One pair of lady's carpet slippers in blue velvet with dollar-sign motif and legend "Good Luck from Macey's" picked out in gold silk. *Estimate: £275,000.*

Lot 3. A similar lot to above in red with label attached — "Do Not Remove. Property of the Excelsior Hotel, Grand Bahamas". *Estimate: £230,000.*

Lot 4. One Banjo (by Hobbs & Verity of Fifeshire) with two strings missing. Certificate of authenticity confirming it was played by the Duke to entertain members of Hitler's staff at Buckingham Palace in 1933. No case. *Estimate: £148,000 (as illustrated).*

Lot 5. Very fine Fishnet Basque with Garter Ensemble in Scarlet Satin. As worn by the Duchess during her stay at Claridges (1953). *Estimate: 12p.*

Lot 6. Highly important unopened copies of Punch Magazine. Still in wholesaler's wrapping. Rare copies from 1996 to 1997.

Lot 7. A similar lot.

Lots 8-973. Similar lots.

NEW YORK – PARIS – NEASDEN

The Daily Hurleygraph

British Actress Has Picture Taken

by Our Entire Staff CHARLES COR, AUBERON WHOAR and SIR PEREGRINE PHWOARSTHORNE

A TOP British actress, Miss Elizabeth Hurley, 23, wore a dress when she went out last night.

Our photograph shows her wearing the dress, which other newspapers have been reluctant to print on their front pages.

We have no such reservations. Cor! Look at her, lads! Blimey! Wouldn't you?

Get a load of that! Phwoar!

Leading Article: Page 17
Letters Page: 18
Comment by W.F. Deedesh: Page 19

SPRING BOOKS

The By-Pass Through The Willows

by Kenneth Grahamotorway

"Poo-poo," said Toad

CLASSIC children's tale of how the car-mad Toad wants to drive all over the countryside on vast dual carriageways. Mole bravely goes underground with his friends "Animal" and "Swampy" to protest against the scheme, but the weasels are in Government and they send in the stoats to flush the little creatures out. Look out for the unhappy ending. Not suitable for children.

Alternative Rocky Horror Service Book

No. 94. A Service Of Induction For A Lady Priest As Canoness-Prebend Of St Paula's Cathedral

President (the Dean, for it is he): Brothers and Sisters, we are gathered here together to induct our sister Lucy Twinkey as a fully-qualified Canoness and Lady Prebenderette of this cathedral. If anyone present knows of any just cause or impediment why this woman should not be on the front page of the Times tomorrow morning, let them squeak now or forever hold their handbags.

All: We object.

President: On what grounds?

All: She's a woman, you fool!

(There will then be a reading from the feminist bible, Good News For Modern Woman)

"And Jesus chose unto himself twelve apostles who were all men, which was typical of the phallocentric tyranny of those times, And he said unto them: "Verily, I say unto you, by the year 2000, things will be very different. Mark my words." Here ends the reading.

RESPONSES

President: Why art thou all leaving?

All: Because we have had it up to here with these ghastly women.

President: You're not really going to go, are you?

All: Yes, we jolly well are.

President: Let us pray.

All: No, we're off.

(At this point the rest of the canons shall process out in an orderly queeny huff. Then the newly-inducted Canoness Twinkey shall lead what remains of the congregation in the following chorus from the Frank Sinatra Hymn Book accompanied by herself on the guitar)

Rev. Twinky: She's not too hungry for Communion at 8. She loves her Matins, and never comes late.
She believes in forgiveness, for people she hates.
That's why the lady is a priest.
© Rodgers and Sacred Hart.

All (Verger): Amen.

"Yes, anti-road campaigning has been good to him"

Video Releases of the Week

Around The World In Five Minutes

Classic star-packed British adventure comedy, in which intrepid explorer Silliarse Branson sets off on a heroic publicity stunt by flying a hot-air balloon onto the front pages of every newspaper in the world. Hilarious climax as balloon takes off and immediately comes down again, nearly killing everyone on board.

Cast in full

Richard Branson	CHARLES BRONSON
Per Lindstrom	MAX VON SYDOW
Man on Camel	DAVID FROST
"Dirty Tricks Squad"	THE STAFF OF BRITISH AIRWAYS (prop. Sir C. Marshall)

Those Magnificent Men In Their Flying Balloons

Classic star-packed British adventure farce about international round-the-world balloon race. The fun starts when all the balloons crash to the ground minutes after take-off, nearly killing everyone on board.

If You Have Tears To Shed...

It was the incomparable Bard of Avon himself, if I am not mistaken, which those who know me are kind enough to say I never am, who with his customary gift for the *mot juste* hit the proverbial nail on the equally proverbial head when he wrote of the death of Levinius Pontificus in that much under-rated masterpiece *Bernardo, the Bore of Wapping*, that when the great man departed from the earth:

The heavens themselves did rend apart
And shower sad rain upon the grieving world,
Yea, e'en the very bees did moan in tuneful dirge
As with dull wings they toiled upon the bud;
And in the streets the children wailed their song,
That one was gone who once had been their king;
Remembering heart-spent in doleful rhymes
The greatest-ever column in the Times.

There will doubtless be those churlish souls, Mr Enoch Powell among their number, and their number grows apace with every year, that our schoolchildren must spend their days poring over the texts of soap operas and sociological tracts rather than on the proper study of mankind which is, as the poet said, man himself, there will, as I say, be those who stoutly maintain, or thinly maintain for all I know, or indeed care, that the author of this incomparable tribute to arguably the greatest writer who has ever bestridden the narrow columns of the Times like a colossus, was not Shakespeare, or Shagspaw as some pedants urge, or even Shakazulu for aught I know or for that matter care, or have I said this before?, not that I am going to allow this to worry me now, for it never has in the past, nor will it in the future (*There is no future. You're fired. Ed*). You will never see my like again (*You're still fired. Ed*). As I was saying before I was so rudely interrupted (*Come in Bernard Levin, you're time is up. Ed*) O tempora, O mores, or for those without the inestimable benefits of a classical education, oh dear the Times seems to have sacked me. (*Not to be continued*)

Bernard Levin

TIME FOR LONGFORD TO BE RELEASED says everybody

by Our Crime Staff Charles Moores-Murders

A PETITION bearing over 30 million signatures was yesterday presented to God, calling for the immediate release of Lord Longford from any further imprisonment in his earthly state.

"Isn't 90 years enough for this poor old man?" said one petitioner, Lady Longford, 94, from her Sussex home.

"Whatever he has done, surely he has paid his debt to society and he should be let out at once."

Lord Longford is 203.

LETTERS TO THE EDITOR

Sir, As usual I have compiled my customary list of the year's most popular christian names from the Births columns of the Times newspaper. The results are as follows:

Boys
1. Buzz; 2. Imran; 3. Taki; 4 Sebag-Montefiore; 5. Del; 6. Tel; 7. Mel; 8. Prince Charles; 9. Van der Post; 10. Peregrine Worsthorne

Girls
1. Tara; 2. Jemima; 3. Spice; 4. Bel; 5. Shel; 6. Mel; 7. Victoria Coren; 8. Madame Vasso; 9. Esther; 10. Lady Lucinda Lampton

I remain
Yours faithfully
ARNOLD E. SCHWARZENEGGER (OBE)
The Old Nuthouse, Nr Bath.

The Daily Tudorgraph

Ye Plans For Ye New Royal Shippe Hailed By All Ye Populace

HIS gracious Majesty King Henry Ye Eighth hath announced ye immediate building of a wondrous new craft for himself to be paid for by a

by Our Politicking Staff
SIR CHARLES MOORE

grateful public.

"It shall be a symbol of ye nation's pride," he quoth, "and

shall reflect ye standing of ye monarch as he shall sail around ye known world."

He continued to quoth: "Ye ship shall be named ye 'Mary Rose'." *(Continued 1594)*

Last Night of the Conservatives

Rule Britannia,
Britannia rules the waves.
Britons never, never, never
Shall pay for another one.

(Traditional)

Exclusive To All Newspapers

MAN IN BRACES CHANGES JOB

by Our Media Staff **Phil Space**

A MAN in shirt sleeves and red braces is to give up his job and get another one, it was revealed today.

The news sent a shock wave through the whole of the newspaper industry, who immediately put the story on the front page.

No one knows why the man has left his job, nor what he is going to do next, nor does anyone care.

But speculation was rife last night over who might succeed the man in braces in doing whatever it is he has been doing for the last few years.

Insiders were predicting that his successor would be:

● a man with a beard

● a woman
● a man with glasses, or
● a woman with a beard.

All are highly experienced and supremely qualified to succeed the man with braces as he goes off to do something or other for even more money.

ON OTHER PAGES

■ Tributes pour in to the man they call "The man in red braces".

■ Two minutes' silence in TV studios as braces man bows out.

■ Major declares national holiday to mark Red Braces Day.

COURT CIRCULAR

The Prince of Wales will today attend the Rumpingdon Hunt, Beds. He will be riding Old Flame and will be met by representatives of the international press corps including Signor Slizi Giornali from the Italian magazine *Lecho!* Mr Kevin Orrid of the *Sun* newspaper and Monsieur Jean-Paul Longue-Lènse from the best selling French periodical *UK Titz et Bumz*. They will attempt to take his photograph alongside Mrs Camilla Parker-Bowles but will be disappointed.

The Procession of the Hunt will be as follows:

1st Horse
HRH The Prince of Wales, on Old Flame.

2nd Horse (½ Hour Later)
HRH Camilla, Princess of Highgrove on Naughty Boy.

3rd Horse
Brigadier Sir Rumswell Rednose KGB, OMC, PG, HGV, DVLC, RSVP on Punch Drunk.

1st Hound
Tyson

2nd Hound
O.J. Simpson

3rd Hound
Von Bulow

1st Fox
Edward

1st Saboteur
Mr Dave Beard

2nd Saboteur
Miss Sarah Anorak

1st Policeman
Inspector Knacker, Bedfordshire Anti-Saboteur Armed Response Unit

1st Range Rover
Miss Tamara Puree-Pilkington; Miss Santa Barbara Trilby Tompson; Miss Tasmina Fanta Lemonade-Beckworth Smythe. *(That's enough. Ed)*

"Must you always go topless on the beach?"

Mother Golden Goose

There was an old woman who lived in a bank.
She had so much money she did not know who
to thank.
At the age of 35 she had five young kiddies.
And for some unknown reason, she earned one
million quiddies.

(Traditional English Rhyme)

School news

St Cake's

'Flu Term begins today. There are 409 boys in the sanatorium. Ben Ilyn-Original (Lemsip's) is Head Ache. Miss Anna Din (Meggozone's) is Night Nurse. Mr T.C.P. Mouthwash takes over all classes until the remainder of the staff are well enough to resume their duties. Strepsils will be given out on Beecham's Powder on Feb 24th. The Contact 2000 Centre will be opened on March 1st by Miss Cherry Tunes O.C. There will be a performance of The Fisherman's Friend by Benjamin Britten in the Lockets Room on March 15th (tickets from the Bursar, Major John Asprin-all, Tiger House, Deadkeepers' Lane). Expectorants will be on March 21st.

"Oh no! Junkie mail!"

Extraordinary Talent Lost To Public Service Broadcasting

SIR CHRISTOPHER Evans was the most outstanding broadcaster of his generation, **writes Phil Space**, and his departure from Radio One will leave an empty void that cannot be filled by lesser mortals.

His career, spanning as it does several weeks, stretches from his early days on Greater Neasden Radio where he coined his immortal catchphrase ("I want more money") to the lofty heights of BBC Radio One's Breakfart Show where he coined another immortal catchphrase ("I want more money and more holidays").

Sir Chris single-handedly pioneered a wholly new genre in the field of popular broadcasting and his innovative style made him easily recognisable to listeners. Who but Sir Crass could have come up with radio formats such as

● Honk if you're on the bog
● Honk if you've got a big one
● Honk if you want a bonk
● Honk if you want a honk
and
● I'm not coming in to work today?

He now takes his place in the pantheon of radio immortals alongside such legendary figures as Simon Dead, Dave Lee Trousers and various others you have forgotten.

Distressed callers meanwhile jammed the lines at Radio One only to be greeted by a recorded message on Sir Croesus's personal ansaphone which said:

"I am not prepared to answer this call until you give me a million pounds and 12 weeks holiday".

Such an approach has already revolutionised the whole ansaphone outgoing message industry and it

seems inevitable now that Sir Christopher will be given a special plaque in Westminster Abbey alongside Tony Blackburn and Dave "Diddy" Hamilton *(Who they? Ed.)* and his name will live for ever *(continued 94FM)*

MEDICAL BRIEFING
◆
Dr Thomas Stuttaford

Facing Life Without Work

Not working can often prove to be as dangerous as working for today's highly stressed top earners. The experience of both Nichola Horlick and Christopher Evans teach us nothing at all but the editor has asked me to fill up some space with one of my little pieces, so here it is.

GOVERNMENT ATTACKS 'SCOTTISH BEGGARS'

by Our Home Affairs Staff Tam O'Ranter

AN ASTONISHING outburst by a government minister, Mr McLoony, caused a storm today when he called for a policy of "Zero Tolerance" on unemployed Scottish beggars.

"These no-hopers," he said, "hang around outside the House of Commons and threaten people who do not give them their vote.

"They may attract sympathy with their sad faces and pathetic hard-luck stories," he continued, "but I can assure you that they are highly organised and potentially dangerous."

Big Tissue Of Lies

The minister then named a number of beggars, all of whom he claimed came from Scotland.

"Tony is one," he declared, "who smiles at everyone in a winning way but who should not be trusted.

"Wee Gordon is another typical scrounger, and so is his friend Auld Cookie, who has a beard and wild staring eyes.

"I am sickened by them all!" he shouted. "One of them even has a dog to attract sympathy. He's called MacBlunkett and you'd better steer clear of him."

The Minister warned the public not to listen to the Scotsmen's aggressive begging and told voters to vote Conservative or else they would be beaten up.

"We know where everyone in the country lives," he said. "So make the right decision."

Mr Maclean is 42.

HORLICK
for sound dreamless sleep

If you are having trouble going to sleep, open your newspaper and help yourself to a stomachful of rich boring Horlick.

Within minutes the soothing whine of Horlick will send you into a deep satisfying slumber.

Horlick – For Working (And Out Of Work) Supermums Everywhere

Ingredients: 40% PR; 10% Artificial Sweetener; 50% Sour Grapes and Hard Cheese. **Price: £1 million.**

Mmmm! Z-z-z...

(Warning: Fishy smell and unpleasant taste may be left in mouth)

PROFILE

Two Scottish beggars who went home

TWO typical Scotsmen who were initially attracted to the bright lights of London have taken the Minister's recent advice and returned to Bonny Scotland, writes the Eye's Insight Team, **Phil Space.**

Case History One – Andrew "Wee Andy" Jaspan

Like many of his countrymen, Andy was lured to the capital by the promise of easy money. A kind-hearted English benefactor Peter Preston, who ran a small business in London's seedy Farringdon Road, offered Andy a job editing the Observer. Little did the charitable old philanthropist know what havoc Jaspan was about to wreak. Within days the place was in ruins and Jaspan was out on the street. He now sells the Big Issue in Scotland.

Case History Two – Andrew "Brillo" Neill

Like many of his countrymen, Andy was lured to the capital by the promise of easy money. An unpleasant Australian benefactor running a vast international business in London's seedy Wapping offered Brillo a job editing the Sunday Times.

Little did the devious old megalomaniac know what havoc Neill was about to wreak. Within ten years the Sunday Times was a byword for all that was worst in British journalism. Brillo was thrown out on the street. He now sells the European back in Scotland.

Neill and Jaspan after losing their shirts

SHAME OF VICE GIRL CAUGHT WITH TORY MP

by Our Political Staff
Lunchtime O'Penairsex

A 17-YEAR-OLD Soho hostess wept last night as her career as a top slapper lay in ruins after revelations about her association with a 47-year-old member of Parliament.

"I am so ashamed," Miss Cocks told reporters brandishing cheque books "I can't believe I went off for a grope in the park with a Tory MP. It was a moment of sheer madness.

"I have made a terrible mistake," Miss Cocks admitted, "but my pimp is standing by me and I just hope the vice community can find it in their hearts to forgive this one indiscretion."

The MP, Mr Piers Pornmerchant, was unapologetic last night.

"What did she expect? I'm a Tory MP! She must have known what she was letting herself in for. What a fool!"

Miss Cocks may still be forced to resign from her post at the Pussies 'R Us Executive Relief Club in Dean Street.

Said the furious owner, Mr Slizi Weezy: "I have no comment to make at present. I will have to consult the committee on the damage that Miss Cocks's actions have done to the reputation of the club. Her previous record as a first-rate local scrubber, however, will be taken into account."

John Major is finished.

"And you must be Sleazy!"

GENERAL ERECTION SPECIAL

BIT ON THE OUTSIDE

This is another Tory cock-up

CONSERVATIVE BALLS

Fancy a Gay Gordon?

Where is he?

MP KISSES WIFE SHOCK

Happy Darling?

Very, you shit

MORE TORY BALLS

Do you want a safe seat?

Where is he?

BLAIR CALLS FOR END TO FOCUS ON SLEAZE

by Our Election Staff
Phil Space

LAST night Mr Tony Blair called for a return to "proper political debate about the real issues that ordinary people are concerned about".

"Let us," he said, "forget once and for all the bribes taken by Mr Hamilton and Mr Smith, the question mark hanging over Mr Merchant after his sex act with a seventeen-year-old prostitute in the park, the homosexual liaison of the Chairman of the Scottish Conservative Party. Let us not dig up old stories about the adulterous Mr Mellor, the 3-in-a-bed Mr Spring or 2-in-a-bed gay love-romp of Mr Ashby in a sleazy French Hotel. No, we will not stoop so low as to resurrect Mr Parkinson's sad affair with his researcher or even tell again the disastrous tale of Mr Profumo and Miss Mandy Rice *(continues for several hours)*"

YES IT'S THE SPACE GIRLS!

by Our Home Affairs Correspondent **Phil Spice**

NOW it's official! The fabulous five-member all-girl group have taken the world of newspapers by storm.

This week they were voted The Best Way To Fill Space by all of Britain's top editors!

Said Charles Moore, editor of the Daily Mel-B-graph: "The Space Girls are the best thing that has ever happened to us. They are going to be really huge — about ten column inches on every page!"

He continued: "I predict they will be top of the news agenda for a long time to come."

The girls' undemanding brand of Britpap has meant that every editor has a copy of the latest Space Girls press release on his desk.

And the Space Girls, known in the newspaper business as Large Space, Huge Space, Vast Space, Op-Ed Space and Front Page Space, have proved they have a unique talent.

"When it comes to showing their knickers, these girls are world beaters", said Peter Stoddart of the unpop fanzine the Times.

Melinda Messenger is yesterday's news.

CASH FOR JOKES SCANDAL
Fayed gave 'huge sums'

by Our Media Staff **James Sleaze-Milne**

THE Egyptian-born businessman Mr Mohamed Al-Fayed was today revealed to have given "thousands of pounds" to a number of prominent journalists in the belief that he would receive "jokes" in return.

But instead the hacks merely pocketed the money and went out for expensive lunches. The beneficiaries included **Mr Stewart Steven**, who received over £200,000 as well as lavish refurbishments to his luxury Wiltshire home; **Mr Peter McHackey**, who received an estimated £175,000 much of it described as "expenses" and **Mr Paul Spike**, an American, who received 35p.

Punch Drunk

All three men deny that there was any kind of deal with Mr Fayed.

"I never had any intention of providing jokes for Mr Fayed," said a spokesman for all three men. "He was just a very generous man who occasionally gave us large cheques because he was that sort of person."

Mahood Al Fayed

An angry Mr Fayed yesterday told reporters "These f***ing bastards have taken my f***ing money. Where are my f***ing jokes?."

A spokesman for Mr Fayed, Mr Mohammed Cole, translated his employer's remarks as follows: "Mr Winston Churchill Fayed is a very upright and patriotic English gentleman whose only desire is to restore standards of humour to public life."

Cooking The Books
with Michel Roux

Ingredients:

400,000 pounds of money

2 pension funds

1 chef

Put the money in one pension fund then, after a while, put it in another one but don't tell the Revenue.

CAUTION: This recipe may burn your fingers

THE VICE GIRLS

We've got what you want.. what you really really want....

And what do you do?

We make you look a prat

IT'S QUIET.... TOO QUIET...

NICHOLAS

Lines Written On The Investiture of Sir Paul McCartney OM as a Knight of the Realm

by William Rees Maccagonagall

'Twas in the year nineteen hundred and ninety-seven
That the great Paul McCartney thought he had gone to
heaven
When he was summoned to the Palace by Her Majesty
the Queen
In a chauffeur-driven German-made limousine.

Incidentally this was not the first time that Paul had set
foot in that hallowed place,
But on the previous occasion his visit had ended in disgrace.
For when he, along with his fellow Beatles, received the MBE
They afterwards boasted they had smoked cannabis in
the Royal WC.

In those days Sir Paul cut a very different dash.
He spent most of his days making cakes filled with hash.
This was whilst recording songs like Let It Be
Whilst under the influence, it was claimed, of LSD.

But then young Paul embarked on a search for Nirvana
Which led him to India but not to Ghana.
He sat at the feet of a bearded holy man
Who told him "Hand over as much money as you can."

While he sat at the Maharishi's feet
He decided it was time for him to stop eating meat.
And thus he met the woman who was to become his wife
And they agreed to eat vegetarian burgers for the rest of
their life.

Thus reformed, Paul settled down near Rye
To live off his royalties which were considerably high.
Here he farmed in an environmentally-friendly style
While songs like Mull of Kintyre continued to add to his
pile.

And so it came to pass that in Paul's old age
The nation came to see him as a venerable sage.
And Mr Major, hoping to win the next election,
Included Sir Paul in his New Year Honours selection.

The Queen herself dubbed him with her shining sword
(Though Lloyd-Webber did better and was made a Lord).
But alas for John Major, despite creating Sir Paul,
On May first, he still ended up getting no votes at all.

©W. Rees-MacGonagall

"I only said you could get your ears pierced"

Alternative Rocky Horror Servicebook

No. 94: Service For The Giving Of Arms In Return For Money (for St Paul's only)

President:	Who sponsoreth this event?
Chairman of Lockheed (*or it may be some other manufacturer of deadly weapons*)**:**	I doeth.
President:	Blessed are the arms makers.
Congregation:	For they shall make arms.
President:	Give war in our time O Lord.
Congregation:	Because that is the way we maketh our money.
President:	O Lord, open thou our lips.
Congregation:	And we shall receive free canapés and champagne in the hospitality area.
	(All face the hospitality area which was formerly the altar. There shall then follow a suitable anthem. It may be Handel's Music for the Royal Firearms or the theme tune from Guns of Navarone)
Canon:	I am a canon.
All:	You're fired. Ha ha ha.

© Carey and Sharey Productions plc

A Taxi-Driver writes

Every week a well-known Member of Parliament is asked to comment on an issue of national importance.

This week **Dave Evans** (Cab No. 4271)

Blimey, I'll tell you who's really stupid, guv. That Mrs Bottomley. Dead from the neck up. That's what I call her. The only reason thcy give her a job is cos she's a woman. They can't even park a car. Look at that silly cow over there in 'er jeep. And I'll tell you another thing. Them blacks that come over 'erc to live on the social security. Rapists and murderers, every one of 'em. They're all guilty, just like the Bridgewater Five and the Birmingham Three. They all did it, you can tell. They were all Irish, weren't they? Or black? Or were they women? Anyway, you can't have women in politics, can you? It's never been the same since they got rid of Maggie. God bless 'er. Know who I had in the back of the cab once? Danny Baker. He's a real gentleman. No, he's a very clever man. Do you want a receipt? No, have a load of them, fill 'em in yourself. Be lucky.

NEXT WEEK: **Dave Maclean** *(cab. no. 74317) on why Roisin McAliskey and her baby should be strung up since it is the only language they understand.*

"Harold's too mean to install a proper cat flap"

Every week **Dave Spart**, Head of English at the John Mortimer Comprehensive, Ealing, and co-chair of the Ex-ILEA Teachers Against Teaching Cooperative, writes on the story behind the news.

THE totally sickening sight of so-called socialist David Blunkett paying lip service to Thatcherite neo-fascist educational elitism, ie standards, inspections and tests which are totally alien to any meaningful learning environment, er… what we demand as professional pedagogic operatives is a) the immediate sacking of the Chief Inspector of Schools, a known fascist and Thatcherite stooge, c) the disbanding of so-called OFSTED which is a totally irrelevant and outmoded institution and 3) the total and utter dismantlement of the Assisted Places scheme, er… the failure to comply with the above forementioned conditions as laid down above to result in an immediate withdrawal of labour, ie, er… a strike and furthermore the television programme "Chalk" is a total insult to the teaching profession suggesting as it does that teachers are illiterate and incompetent which proves this programme is total and utter crap, real crap, I mean *(continued p.94)*

That Liam and Patsy Wedding Breakfast in full

Coke

— ✳ —

Coke

— ✳ —

Coke

— ✳ —

To follow:
Slice of Wedding Coke

— ✳ —

To drink:
Coke

The bride will enter to the tune of "The Cokey-Cokey" (arranged A. Dealer). The guests will have a traditional English nose-up. (Surely some mistake? Ed).

TORIES ENNOBLE LORD WEBBER

It's in recognition of your remarkable gifts

Yes, very generous of you

49

Daily Mail

FRIDAY, APRIL 4, 1997   35p

YES, IT'S TONY BL-IRA!

by Our Political Staff
"Sir" Paul Dacre, Conservative candidate for a peerage

LABOUR leader Tony Blair is hand-in-glove with the mass-murderers of the IRA and may even have personally planted the notorious Wilmslow bomb, the *Mail* can reveal.

A highly-placed source (Michael Howard) has told the *Daily Mail* that Mr Blair's repeated refusal to support the Prevention of Terrorism Act was clear evidence of his membership of the General Army Council of the world's most sinister terrorist organisation.

Labour was sent reeling last night when further revelations in today's *Daily Mail* uncovered a secret Labour plot to hand over the running of Britain to the unions, led by Arthur Scargill.

Vote Tory

A very highly placed source indeed (Baroness Thatcher) last night told the *Daily Mail:* "It will be just like the winter of discontent all over again, with corpses lying unburied in the streets, being gnawed by rats."

Major leaps ahead in poll upset

LABOUR leader Tony Blair was yesterday in tears when an opinion poll in today's *Daily Mail* showed that John Major now has a commanding 90% lead in a key poll.

At Tory Central Office champagne corks were popping as a jubilant Dr Mawhinney held up a copy of the poll but refused to show it to anyone.

NOTE: The Tori poll was conducted on a random sample of 5 committed Tory voters.

IRA TO HIRE STAGECOACH SHOCK

by Our Railway Staff **John Le Carriage**

FOLLOWING the failure of their attempt to bring Britain's railways to a halt by blowing up the signal box at Wilmslow, Cheshire, the IRA are now planning a much more daring assault on the nation's train system.

The General Council of the IRA, we can reveal, is planning to approach Mr Brian Souter, the head of Stagecoach, asking him to take over the entire rail network.

"If he can do to the rest of the system what he's already done to the South West," said spokesman Mr Shameless O'Semtex, "then we are home and dry."

YOUR TRAINS TONIGHT

All cancelled owing to the wrong type of management

"Achilles! Those heels will be the death of you!"

MASS SUICIDE OF BIZARRE CULT ROCKS NATION

by Our Political Staff **Harry Kiri and Sandy Ego**

IN THE early hours of yesterday morning the City of Westminster woke up to the horrific reality that 324 Tories had committed mass suicide.

All the members of a strange fanatical sect calling themselves the Conservative Party were found in identical uniforms of pinstripe suit and blue rosette.

"They were all lying," said a shocked observer. "Lying all over the House of Commons. It was horrible and the stink was unbearable."

Sect Scandal

Why these men committed political suicide is still unknown but the blame may rest with their leader, a greying 50-year-old who exercised an unhealthy influence over his followers.

Higher HP Source

Said a shocked observer: "It's incredible. They all seemed perfectly respectable men going about their business and then suddenly we discover that they all had a death wish."

The motive for this final act of self-destruction is a mystery. Some experts point to financial greed, others to sexual lust, others to staggering all round incompetence.

"No one could stop them," said one expert. "They were determined to end it all. And they did."

Radio Four

What you missed...

The Today Programme

Sue MacGhastly: ...and the news is just coming in, I'm delighted to say, that a bomb has gone off in Wilmslow, and we're going over to Ken Stiggis who is on the spot, only six miles down the motorway. Ken, what can you tell us?

Stiggis: Well, Sue, from what I've just heard on the *Today Programme*, there's been a bomb explosion in Wilmslow.

MacGhastly: Do we have any details yet about how many people might be injured and how badly?

Stiggis: No, Sue, they haven't said anything about that on the radio.

MacGhastly: So you can't even give us any figures about the number of people who haven't been injured?

Stiggis: It's really too early to give you any figures, Sue.

MacGhastly: Any eyewitness reports of bodies flying through thee air, or scenes of indescribable horror?

Stiggis: No, Sue, unfortunately not.

MacGhastly: Well, we'll keep you informed so that you can tell us what's going on in time for the 8 o'clock News. And now it's time for Thought for the Day from Mr Kelvin Bairnsfather who is a reader in Satanic Studies at the Beelzebub Institute in Slough.

Bairnsfather: Sitting in the studio just now, I heard the terrible news of the massacre in Wilmslow, and my heart went out to all the families who have been so cruelly blown up by this heartless act. But we Satanists have a saying, which my old auntie Wanda always used to quote, that if you just whistle a happy tune, all your troubles will go away. Thank you Sue, thank you Jim.

MacGhastly: Thank you, Kelvin. And we're just getting news of a mass-suicide in America. There must be dead there, surely?

Humphrys: Ha, ha, ha.

MacGhastly: We haven't got any details yet, but that's not going to stop us. We're going over now to Ken Stiggis in Wilmslow. What can you tell us about this mass-suicide, Ken?

Stiggis: Well, Sue, apparently a lot of people have died in America. We're still a little in the dark about how many bodies there are, and whether they're flying through the air, or just lying in neat rows on the ground. As soon as I hear anything more I'll let you know.

Humphrys: And now, the 8 o'clock news.

Brian Perkins *(for it is he):* On this programme just now, it was reported that a lot of people are dead in America but that Ken Stiggis doesn't know much more about it... *(Continued for 94 minutes)*

Stories Retold From The Bible No. 94

The Conversion of St Andrew

NOW there was a holy man at that time whose name was A.N. Wilson. And he dwelt in Oxford, where he wrote many learned books concerning the law and the prophets. And he was a devout man, known for his piety and his devotion to his tweed suit and bicycle clips. But Andrew was a poor man and his improving tracts had few sales and even fewer readers.

Then one day St Andrew went on a journey to his publisher who was called St Clair of Stevenson, another holy man. And suddenly, as he was on the road, there came to him a vision, like unto a blinding flash. And he heard a voice saying: "Andrew, Andrew, why don't you persecute me?"

And when Andrew recovered from the vision, his eyes were opened and he realised that everything he had believed all his life was a load of rubbish. And from that day forth, he preached against the Gospel of Jesus and became the richest of all the scribes.

© Society for the Propagation of Atheist Knowledge

CHANNEL 5
What you will see

A Doctor writes

AS a Doctor, I am often asked: "Are you HIV positive?"

The short answer is: "Yes I am, but I am not going to tell anyone because I would lose my job."

If you're worried about being HIV positive, keep very quiet and then leave the country.

© A Doctor

The Privatised Underground

Your cut-out-'n'-keep guide to the new-look Tube

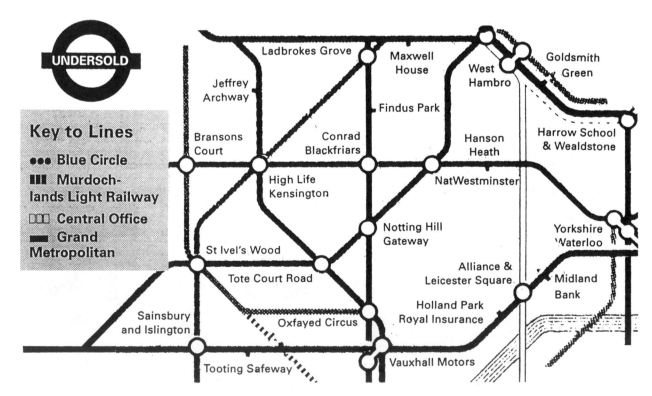

UNDERSOLD

Key to Lines

- ●●● **Blue Circle**
- ▮▮▮ **Murdoch-lands Light Railway**
- ▯▯▯ **Central Office**
- ▬ **Grand Metropolitan**

Ladbrokes Grove · Maxwell House · West Hambro · Goldsmith Green

Jeffrey Archway · Findus Park

Bransons Court · Conrad Blackfriars · Hanson Heath · Harrow School & Wealdstone

High Life Kensington · NatWestminster

Notting Hill Gateway · Yorkshire Waterloo

St Ivel's Wood · Alliance & Leicester Square · Midland Bank

Tote Court Road

Sainsbury and Islington · Oxfayed Circus · Holland Park Royal Insurance

Tooting Safeway · Vauxhall Motors

COURT CIRCULAR

BUCKINGHAM PALACE

Her Majesty the Queen granted an audience to Mr Stephen Mannorak, representing the firm Webs-'R-Us, in order to launch the new Royal Web site. She has graciously consented to receive ER-mail at brenda@buck-house.stuffDi.maj.uk.

HIGHGROVE

Her Queen-in-Waitingness, Lady Camilla Parker-Knowles, gave a televisual audience with Mr Chris Crass from Channel 5 as part of a series of commercials to launch a new-look Camilla — "Soft, caring, gentle, and not a horsey old baggage who has run off with the Heir to the Throne."

YABBA-DABBA-DUBAI

His Royal Highness the Prince of Wales arrived here today on the Royal Yacht HMS Floating Trade Centre (formerly Britannia). A reception was held on board for His Highness to meet representatives of the local armaments community. Contracts worth £800 billion were exchanged, while the Band of the Royal Marines played a selection from *Ali Get Your Guns*.

SOUTHYORK, SUNNINGDALE

Her Non-Royal Highness Sarah the Duchess of Fergiana took up residence in the Servants' Wing with the Princesses Fifi Trixibelle and Lulu. Following an audience with His Royal Highness Prince Andrew, the following statement was issued: "Although the Duke and Duchess have agreed to cohabit for financial reasons, there will be no carnal relations between the Royal Couple unless the Duchess gets desperate." The Duchess of Fergiana will later attend the transportation of her personal effects to the Servants' Wing and she will be escorted by the staff of Budget Removals led by Mr Sid Clumsy and Mr Len Smash. Also assisting the Duchess will be Mr Smash's half-brother Doug and his mate "Spud". The procession will be as follows:

FIRST VAN

Her Ex-Royal Highness the Duchess of Freebiana; Mr Smash; Mr Clumsy; 200,000 unsold copies of "Budgie Goes Bankrupt".

SECOND VAN

Doug; Spud; the Editor of Hello! Magazine; one million unsold videos of "Budgie Goes Back To Her Husband".

1ST MAN HIDING IN WARDROBE

Mr Johnny Bryan.
(That's enough. Ed.)

That Dudley Moore Panto in full

(Enter Dudley Moore dressed as a Bell-Boy)

Dudley: Hello boys and girls!

Audience: Who are you?

Dudley: I'm Bottles!

Audience: Don't you mean Buttons?

Dudley: I'm going to tell the ugly sisters that they need therapy. Then I'm going to marry Cinderella, divorce her and give her all my money. Finally, I'm going to let Prince Charming live with her in my house.

Audience: Booo!!

Dudley: What do you think of my new career?

Audience: It's behind you!

Dudley: Oh no, it isn't!

Audience: Oh yes, it is!

Dudley: Oh yes, it is *(continues for several hours)*.

BEACHED WALES STILL STRANDED

by Our Environment staff **Herman Melvin Bragg**

THOUSANDS of people yesterday lined the shore of Highgrove estuary to witness the sad spectacle of Mopy the Wales as it tried desperately to find a way back into public favour.

For months a team of experts have been trying to refloat Mopy, when he became grounded after taking a number of wrong turnings on his way to the throne.

Spouting Nonsense

One of those leading the rescue bid, Mr Jonathan Dimbleby said: "We have tried everything — television, books, we have even prayed to Allah — but he remains obstinately stuck in the mud."

Hopes were raised yesterday that Mopy could be coaxed back into the mainstream by the Archbishop of Canterbury, but later Mopy was seen floundering about and lashing out blindly in all directions on the theme of the built environment.

Last night everyone seemed sadly agreed that Mopy the Wales seemed to be washed up forever.

And this is what we do to adulterers...

This Islam is er... awfully good...

CAESAR PLUMPS FOR IDES POLL

by Our Political Staff **Brutus Anderson**

A RELAXED and confident Julius Major today announced that he would be going to the country on the Ides of March.

Brushing aside rumours of splits and plots, the leader said that when it came to the day everyone "would be right behind him".

Senior colleagues stressed that the party was still united and their plans for European unity were well on course. Speeches by Portillus, Heseltinus, Mark Alpinus and Cassius Dorrellius all supported their leader. "We are backing him to the hilt," they said. "Some people say that Caesar's future is on a knife-edge, but nothing could be further from the truth. As we agreed at our backstreet meeting last week: 'We have come to bury Major not to praise him'."

Shockus

Later Dorrellius issued a clarification saying that he had not intended to give the impression that he was going to stab Julius Major in the back. He had been quoted out of context and had meant to say "We come to *murder* Major because he's useless".

ON OTHER PAGES

See-Through Togas — Dare you wear them? IV

Mysticus Megus warns Taureans your unlucky colour is blue V

Appian Way Protest — Swampus strikes again VIII

EYEWITNESS FROM ALBANIA

by Our Man in Tirana
Phil Space

Tuesday

IT IS Tuesday morning in the small village of Nisdina. An old goat walks slowly down the street accompanied by his owner, an elderly woman dressed in a traditional headscarf and pair of trainers. Somewhere a cock crows loud enough to waken the dead. But the dead are not there to be woken.

As an old goat walks slowly down the mainstreet of the once thriving market town of Nisdina, I talk to an old woman, her head shrouded in the traditional scarf of this once-proud country.

With a silent gesture she indicates that she is Kate Adie and she is looking for someone to interview.

In the distance a cock crows. It is Tuesday. But for the Albanians who must live here it is just another day in Albania.

This is Phil Space, in Albania, Tuesday.

© *The Observer*

ARE YOU SURE MY BLIND DATE LOOKS LIKE AN ITALIAN TOY BOY

BESTIE

Exclusive serialisation only in Private Eye

Tim Bell's Dark Secret

by Mark Shillingsworth

Part 94

AS THE 'eighties dawned it became more and more obvious that one of the country's leading coke sniffers had become hopelessly addicted to Mrs Thatcher.

"I was at a meeting where I was trying to discuss a drugs deal," recalls a colleague, "and all Tim would talk about was Thatcher. You couldn't stop him. He couldn't get enough of her. Sure, he pretended he could handle it but it was obvious he was hooked."

Jim Bogleby (of Bogleby Hargle and Pratt) took Bell to one side and told him he should seek help with AA (Admen Anonymous).

But Tim denied he had a problem with Thatcher. "I can take a line of Thatcher," he would tell friends, "but I'm not hooked."

But the truth was Bell was driving down to Downing Street in his Flasharati nearly every day for his fix of "Thatch".

In the end Bell's reputation as a coke-snorting flasher was severely compromised and Tim *(continued page 94)*

VICAR DISCOVERED DOING JOB SHOCK

by Our Religious Staff **Rev Nick Shopping**, team vicar of St Tesco's, Cornwall

A CHURCH of England vicar, the Reverend Goodie, has been discovered carrying out his duties amongst his congregation without attracting publicity of any kind.

Goodie, it was revealed, is neither homosexual nor conducting an adulterous affair with a parishioner's wife. What is more worrying for the church authorities is that he appears to believe in God and has not read any books by A.N. Wilson.

Goodie shocked parishioners recently by preaching against shoplifting, ramraiding, armed robbery and murder, citing only the Ten Commandments in his defence.

There were immediate calls for Goodie to be dismissed, but his Bishop, The Right Rev. Gary Soundbite said: "The C of E is a broad church and there has to be room for people with odd views who do not seek publicity."

EASTER BUNNY 'JUST A MYTH'

by Our Religious Affairs Staff **Peter Pan and Sister Wendy**

THE traditional Easter bunny, beloved of children all over the world, is nothing more than a piece of "babyish gobbledygook".

So says leading religious thinker A.N. Wilson in a new book published today *The Myth Of The Bunny.*

Wilson claims that the bunny was probably a squirrel, an animal common in mediaeval Europe, which became the centre of a cult which was later taken over by Nordic rabbit-lovers who superimposed their own mythology on the original version.

The subsequent addition of supporting religious iconography, including the "Easter Chick", the wearing of bonnets and the ritual consumption of Cadbury's creme eggs, was all just a distortion of the original squirrel cult which flourished in Bohemia from the 12th Century onwards.

"There is no historical proof," Wilson argues, "that the Easter bunny ever hid eggs round people's gardens, and it is utterly babyish to pretend that he did, as a lot of silly Deans would have us believe."

COMING SOON: A.N. Wilson Attacks the Tooth Fairy.

Those new Scouting Badges in full

CAMPING

COTTAGING

CRUISING

BONDAGE

LEATHER WORK

MOUSTACHE

FISTING

MEDICAL BRIEFING

Dr Thomasina Stuttaford

Changing sex

NOWADAYS many doctors feel the need to dress up in women's clothing and change their names. Overnight they will turn from say James Le Fanu to Jemima Le Fanu or Theodore Dalrymple to Theodora Galrymple. There is nothing odd in such behaviour and it does not affect their abilities as doctors to pad out pages of newspapers with articles about anything that is in the headlines. If you are concerned about your doctor changing sex you should try it yourself — perhaps starting with a little cocktail frock or your wife's (continued p.94)

The Daily Cawdorgraph

Price 1 Mickle

Macbeth 'Innocent Till Proven Guilty' says Lady Macbeth

by Our Political Staff Will 'Hutton' Shakespeare

IN THE strife-torn constituency of Glamis and Cawdor Thereafter, the wife of beleaguered Thane Neil Macbeth has intervened to defend her husband.

"There is no evidence to support the allegations that my husband has murdered King Duncan for personal gain," she told a rally of peasants. "In this country, a man is innocent until proved to the contrary, and although my husband has admitted the offence he has yet to be convicted of any misdemeanour."

COME YOU SPIRITS... UNSEAT ME HERE

Lady Christine has often been described as the power behind the throne, and her determination to retain the seat may prove the decisive factor in the campaign for the kingdom.

Meanwhile, the former warrior-correspondent Martin McDuff has declared himself as an "anti-corruption" alternative to Macbeth.

IS THIS A TENNER THAT I SEE BEFORE ME?

"What I'm hoping to do here," he said, "is to mobilise the grass roots of Burnham Wood so that there is a major shift towards Dunsinane. That should finish off Macbeth."

Lady Muck was however unrepentant. She confronted MacBell in his trademark white armour and shouted at him "Out! Out! Damned spotless candidate!"

ON OTHER PAGES

Great Moments in Trainspotting History

Bell Washes Whiter Than White

Yes, it's Martin Bell's doorstep challenge! Would you swap your dirty MP for a bright, clean former war correspondent?

Of course you wouldn't. You're a Tory living in Tatton.

But listen — New Formula Bell is biologically engineered to remove even the toughest sleaze.

Guaranteed to get rid of the following stains:

● **Filthy Fayed** ● **Brown Envelopes** ● **Mixed Grylls**

So, if you can face up to the Bell Doorstep Challenge you can win yourself a candidate who has no idea what he is doing.

Manufactured by LibLab Brothers plc, Staines, Tatton.

Greek Myths Revisited

The Boy Who Flew Too Close To The Sun

TONY BLICARUS was a young boy who was a prisoner in a very old Labour Party. Blicarus longed to be free and to become Prime Minister. So he worked hard and long on making himself a wondrous pair of wings, fashioned from bits and pieces he collected from old speeches by the late Queen Margaret. Finally the day came when Blicarus was able to put on the wings, with the aid of some special wax spun by the clever engineer Mendaedalus. But when Blicarus had donned the wings, Mendaedalus gave his young pupil a solemn warning. "Whatever you do," he said, "don't get too near the Sun, because it will make it too hot, your support will melt and you will come crashing down to earth."

But young Blicarus was a headstrong lad, and he soared up and up in the opinion polls until he nearly reached heaven itself. "It's so blue up here," he shouted, "I can even get close to the Sun."

But even as he spoke the Sun's malign power began to wreak its fateful havoc on those wondrous, see-through wings.

Blicarus suddenly found himself plummeting to earth like a stone, to be lost forever.

© *W.F. Daedalus*

Daily Mail, Friday, April 18, 1997

Why Oh Why Should We Listen To This Self-Important Journalist?

asks Paul Johnson

WHY on earth should anyone take the slightest bit of notice of this ridiculous attempt by a member of the media to intervene in the democratic process?

This man is not a politician, but a mere journalist whose job is to stand on the sidelines, remaining objective like I do, and not tell people to vote for Mr Blair, which they should.

MORE PROZAC PLEASE

Bell is the worst type of BBC creep. Just because he has been in the front line in the Falklands, there is no excuse for him trying to lecture us now on what kind of soup we should eat.

These people in the media are getting completely above themselves.

Some of them are stark, staring mad, as you can tell by just looking at them.

Let us hope that the people of Tatton have the good sense to lynch Mr Bell and string him up for his self-regarding arrogance.

WHERE'S THAT PROZAC?

The thought of some soup-crazed media hireling standing on his soapbox to lay

---

The Afghan Spice Girls

VEILED SPICE | HIDDEN SPICE | MASKED SPICE | COVERED SPICE | OBSCURED SPICE

KELLY

---

down the law about which way to vote is sickening.

In fact it is little short of treason. The only man who can save us now is my old friend Margaret Thatcher.

That is why everyone should vote Labour at this election.

Ask not for whom the Bell tolls. It tolls for me.

Marigold, you can let me out now. I've finished my piece now and I feel a lot better.

Come on, open this door. I've got a gun you know. Don't be a silly girl.

© *The Daily Mail, the Daily Telegraph, the Spectator and all other papers*

TORYTIME:

The Tale of Peter Rabbit

Mrs. Rabbit was a Single Parent. She lived off the state in a sandy bank with her four children.

Peter was Beyond Control. He broke into gardens and stole carrots.

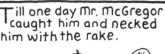

Till one day Mr. McGregor caught him and necked him with the rake.

That's what happens when there's no Father and family meals are not eaten round a table. NB

Lucie was sad. She had lost three pocket handkins and a pinny.

But old Mrs. Tiggy-winkle had taken them and washed, starched and ironed them.

All for FREE!

Thank you kindly, m'm

She didn't whinge about a Minimum Wage. NB

TORYTIME:

The Tale of Mrs. Tiggy-Winkle

TORYTIME:

Rumpelstiltskin

The Queen had to guess Rumpelstiltskin's name.

Alberich?
Bilbo?
Chester?
Darren?
Ed?
Frodo?
Grumpy?
Herman?

She was at her wit's end, till somebody leaked it...

It's Rumpel-stiltskin!

No, it isn't! That was your last chance

...but although caught out, Rumpy managed to brazen it through. NB

The town of Hamelin contracted out its pest control to a Pied Piper.

But the burghers wrangled over payment.

So he led all the town's children away.

IF YOU CAN'T KEEP UP, THEN TOUGH!

Another failure by a Labour-controlled council playing politics with its children's welfare. NB

TORYTIME:

The Pied Piper

TORYTIME: Cinderella

Cinderella wore rags & worked as a servant.

Her stepsisters wore finery & did nothing.

They went to a ball leaving Cinderella behind.

That's about it for Cinderella.

Somebody has to be left behind. NB

TORYTIME: Jack & the Beanstalk

Jack's mother sent him to sell the cow.

Jack sold the cow and bought into beans...

300% RETURN ON CAPITAL...

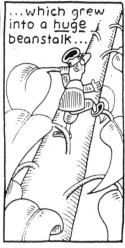

...which grew into a huge beanstalk...

...at the top of which was treasure!

COR, A CASH WINDFALL REPRESENTING A CONSIDER-ABLE RETURN ON INVEST-MENT!

It was tough on the giant whose gold it was, but he had to adapt to economic change. NB

TORYTIME: Adam & Eve

Adam was accused of eating the so-called Apple.

SCOUT'S HONOUR

Eve, his loyal wife, stood by him.

GENESIS HAS A LEFT-WING BIAS

There are more important things than the Fall of man. NB

TORYTIME: Snow White and The Seven Trainee Chefs

Snow White kept house for Seven Dwarfs.

They had been miners but were learning new skills.

Heigh-ho! Heigh-ho! To learn new skills we go...

REAL jobs for REAL people! NB

The Alternative Rocky Horror Service Book

No. 94: A Service Of Outrage For The Embarrassment Of The Church General

The President (*for it is Carey*): Good morning. It's lovely to see so many of you here this morning. First a few notices. The House Group will meet at 7.30 on Tuesday evening at Mountview with Mrs Wetherby (*here he may say 'Mrs Cardew', 'Mrs Lustig' or 'Mrs Finch-Wilkins'*).

Mrs Wetherby (*for it is she*): It's been changed to Tuesday, Your Grace. I've got to take my mother to hospital on Wednesday.

President: Thank you, Joyce. I stand corrected, as ever!

(*The congregation here may laugh or cough politely, to show appreciation of archiepiscopal humour. There shall then be a spontaneous demonstration by members of the Provisional Wing of the Anglican Outrage Movement, coordinated by the Very Irreverent Peter Tatchell*)

Gays: Fascists! Murderers! Closet queens! You're all queers — why don't you come clean like us?

The President: We appreciate your concern and I have appointed a Synodical Commission to investigate this whole area in a very real sense.

Gays: Carey! Carey! Carey! Out! Out! Out!

President: Oh dear. I think we should all sing a hymn now.

(*Gays sing a selection from the 'Oh, Look at Hymnal'*)

THE RESPONSES

Carey: What is it that you want?

Gays: Gay marriage, gay divorce and gay bishops.

Carey: I shall look into it.

Gays: Bastard!

Carey: I'm doing my best.

Gays: Bastard!

Carey: Is there anything else?

Gays: We demand the right of all lesbian fathers to adopt their partners' babies and to conceive by means of artificial insemination.

Carey: It is a matter for Synod.

Gays: Murderer! Pig! You look terrible in purple, dear!

THE DISMISSAL

President: I must now ask you all to depart in peace, or I will have to call the police.

Gays (*very excited at thought of being roughly handled by young men in uniform*): Oooh, see if we care!

Mrs Wetherby: I've just looked at my diary, Reverend, and I see that it's *next* week that I'm taking my mother to hospital. So it's as you were for Tuesday. Can someone bring a pudding?

WHAT YOU MISSED

The Today Programme Radio 4

Humphrys: And now it's time for the weather. More bad news you've got for us, I believe Michael.

Fish: 'Fraid so, John. Another beautiful spring day, with temperatures well into the 20s. That's 80 degrees fahrenheit for old-fashioned listeners. Sun shining everywhere, pleasant light breeze, birds singing, daffodils blooming, and the outlook for the weekend is much the same.

Humphrys: So that's the gloomy story then. By the end of the week there will be widespread drought, huge fires raging uncontrolled all over the countryside, and of course millions of cases of skin cancer, asthma and hay fever. We're going over now to Ken Stiggis, who is in the global warming front line in Burford.

(*Sound of birds singing, lawn mowers whirring and strimmers strimming*)

Humphrys: So, Ken, tell us about the spring terror that is gripping Britain.

Stiggis: It's a scene here of absolute devastation, John. Gardeners I spoke to this morning have never seen anything like it. There's so much cherry blossom that millions of trees could soon be collapsing under the weight.

Sue McGhastly: (*jumping in excitedly*): Could there be any deaths, Ken, as a result of the trees collapsing? Any fatalities or, failing that, horrible injuries to report?

Stiggis: Well, not as yet, Sue, but I've got here the head of the local ambulance service, Mr Barry Stretcher. Mr Stretcher, what plans have you got to cope with the tidal wave of skin cancer victims predicted as a result of this killer spring sunshine?

Stretcher: Good morning.

Stiggis: And what about the hay-fever sufferers? Have you got enough hospital beds to cope with an epidemic of this size?

Stretcher: Er... the Burford Ambulance Service has got a long and proud history of service to the Burford community in the Burford area; and we are confident that we can make a positive response to any demands that are placed on our resources with regard to this one, though there are none to speak of at this present time.

Sue McGhastly: So, it's a far cry then from the days of Wordsworth when he wrote his immortal lines: "Oh to be in England now that spring is here." Today, Wordsworth would find a parched desert filled with people choking to death on the cherry blossom, in the worst outbreak of spring since records began.

If you are worried about any of the effects of this spring catastrophe, you can ring an advice line set up by the Department of Health on 0865-5385000.

Humphrys: I'm afraid there are still no reports of deaths from the cherry blossom, but a man who's got a lot of questions to answer is the man in our Westminster studio, Environment Secretary L. Ron Gummer. Mr Gummer, this appalling spring weather is all your fault and it's going to leave you with blood on your hands, isn't it?

Gummer: Let me begin by saying that this government has spent more money on spring in real terms than... (*Cont'd 94 KHz*)

Men Behaving Baldly

"Oh no! Lopez has fallen asleep at the wheel!"

It's time for a change

I agree. I've just wet myself

Gnome

Reprinted from The Sunday Gnomograph, The Sunday Gnomes, The Gnome on Sunday and others

BLAIR WASHED UP AS LABOUR NOSEDIVE TO POLL OBLIVION

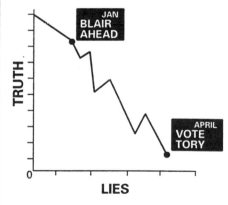

LABOUR's hopes of a general election victory were utterly destroyed yesterday when a new poll revealed that their support had sunk to a disastrous new low. Blair's ailing party is now only a dismal twenty points ahead of the freshly invigorated Conservative Party, whose support has remained firmly unchanged.

There is now nothing for Tony Blair to do except admit defeat with a good grace and wish the Tories the best of luck.

Labour, he *must* realise, are finished. They have run out of ideas. They are finished. They have run out of ideas. They are finished. They have run out of ideas. They are finished.

© Gnome News

How They Will Be Voting

On the eve of poll the Eye team advises readers on how to cast their votes

Dave Spart

GIVEN the sickening lurch of Blair towards the far right and his total and utter betrayal of the working people of Britain, there is only one way to vote on May 1st and that is Labour.

Sir Herbert Gussett

IN OUR part of the country there is only one issue, and that is the takeover of Britain by Herr Kohl's federal superstate. That is why there is only one vote for a loyal patriotic Englishman — The UK Independent Referendum Fish Party, represented in this constituency by the excellent local candidate, whose name temporarily escapes me, but I can assure you that his leaflet is on the hall table behind the pipe rack. I am of course writing this at the local headquarters of the Referendum Party, formerly the Lamb and Flag.

A. Taxidriver

THEY'RE all as bad as each other, aren't they guv? I mean that Major, he's bloody useless, isn't he? He hasn't got a clue. They've never been any good since they threw Maggie out. No, I'm not going to vote for them this time, I'm voting Conservative. I 'ad that Lord Hanson in the back of the cab once. Very clever man.

Glenda Slagg

PADDY ASHDOWN. Don'tcha-lovehim? With his craggy good looks and his penny on income tax, he's top of the polls for me!?! When did Goody Two-Shoes Blair or Measly Major ever show a girl a good time!?! Hi there, Mr Pantsdown, I'll give you a smacking great X on the Libs, geddit?! I won't tell the missus either!?!

Peter McLie, the world's worst columnist and former editor of Punch

HAVE you noticed how quiet all our politicians have gone? The House of Commons is like a morgue these days. No doubt they are all taking advantage of the spring sunshine to take a holiday. Why don't we have a ballot every five years to decide whether they deserve to keep their jobs? I have even thought of a name for such an event — the trouser press!

E.J. Thribb

So. Farewell then
John Major.
I am writing this
Before the result
Is declared.
So I could be wrong.

E.J.T.

A. Doctor

AS a doctor, I am often asked: "Doctor, how do you intend to cast your vote?" The short answer is "Conservative" or *Fundholderus profitensis maximus*, to give it its full medical name.

Gary Bullshit, TV Critic

BLIMEY. Have you seen Dwanda, the new friend of Janine in *EastEnders*? What a pair of honkers! I'd like to give her one! Wouldn't you? Blimey.

"I come from a broken home"

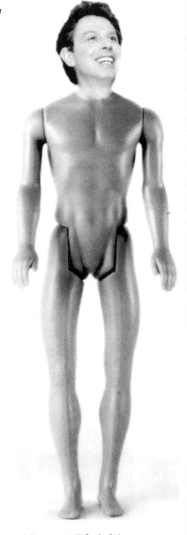

POLL OF POLL OF POLLS

Compiled by Our Political Staff **Phil Space**

How the polls stand

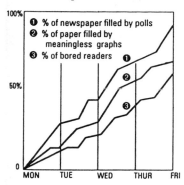

0 % of newspaper filled by polls
2 % of paper filled by meaningless graphs
3 % of bored readers

[X] **64% of the public believe** that Peter Kellner is more boring than Peter Ridell.

[X] 28% want less Paul Johnson than Frank Johnson though 97% wanted neither.

[X] **42% of those polled** thought that Roy Greenslade's election column had even less to say than Brian MacArthur's. However, that is 15% up on last week's poll which indicated that Matthew Parris was 28% duller than Matthew Engel.

[X] Only 2% of those polled had confidence in Peter Preston having anything remotely interesting to say although in the same survey Ferdinand Mount was trailing Preston at 1%, having dropped 39% on his previous 42% lead over Hugo Young whose dull rating remains a steady 73%.

[X] Asked who they would "least like as their leader writer", 97% of the population chose Charles Moore, a swing of 29% away from Dominic Lawson with Will Hutton registering a disappointing 98%, thereby splitting the bored vote three ways.

[X] Asked to name the candidates most likely to lose circulation during the campaign, the survey nominated William Rees-Mogg (53%), Boris Johnson (42%), Petronella Wyatt (41%), Mary Ann Sieghart (27%), W.F. Deedes (21%), Peter Stothart (31%), Peter Kellner *(continued 94%)*

Bar chart update

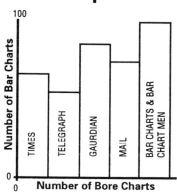

Number of Bar Charts

TIMES, TELEGRAPH, GAURDIAN, MAIL, BAR CHARTS & BAR CHART MEN

Number of Bore Charts

Pre-School Nursery Facility Rhymes

Spin-Doctor Foster went to Gloucester
In a shower of rain.
He stepped in a puddle
Right up to his middle
And then denied it was an error, he
    had always intended to do it,
    and was not a bit wet.

'NO DROUGHT' promise water chiefs

by Our Man Standing In The Reservoir **Keith Waterhosepipeban**

SENIOR executives in the privatised water companies yesterday sought to reassure the public that there would be "no shortage of money" during the summer months.

"We have an ample sufficiency to provide all our needs," said one chairman. "We have vast reservoirs of cash ready to pump straight into our bank accounts. There is no cause for any panic by any director who thinks his money supply might be cut off."

Another chairman agreed. "The money will flow like, well, not water obviously, but like very expensive Napoleon Brandy of the type that I have had sent round to my house this morning.

"A certain amount of money", he admitted, "has been leaking into things like repairs and renovation but I can guarantee that 99% of the dosh is going directly to my accountant in Grand Cayman."

Weather Forecast:
There will be showers of money falling heavily all over the country tonight.

Hot spot:
Thames at £60 million.

MANDELSON UNVEILS NEW LABOUR SYMBOL

by Our Political Staff **Paul Barker**

PETER MANDELSON today hit out at the media for "trivialising the election campaign" and then produced what he called "a sensible and serious gimmick" in order "to try to win a few votes in the run-up to polling day". He then introduced waiting newsmen to a traditional British Bullshit.

"This Bullshit," he said proudly, "is a symbol of the new Labour party. It evokes feelings of passion, patriotism and desperation."

Furious Conservatives attacked Labour's use of the

Bullshit saying: "It's disgusting. When you think of Bullshit, you naturally think of the Tory Party. How dare they steal our image?"

Mr Mandelson, however, defended his strategy. "Voters find Bullshit appealing and in the end that is all that matters. Labour is going through a purple patch at the moment which is a colour that really suits me, don't you think? What's your star sign?"

(Reuters)

Monday

I am on my bus and I am on my way to victory. "No, you're not," said my wife Norman, "you're on your way to Watford." We are going to visit a biro factory for a photo opportunity with Mr Wilmot, who is the managing director. "Change of plan," shouted Mr Dr Mawhinney, who was dressed as a chicken and carrying a number of mobile phones. "The factory's closed down, so we are going to Milton Keynes to launch my new poster saying that Britain is booming." He then presented me with my "new ideas for today".

They were:

1. A grammar school in every town.

2. A grammar school in every school.

3. A grammar school in every motorway service area.

4. A grammar school free with every packet of cornflakes.

5. Mr Blair is cracking up, *unlike me*.

Tuesday

Today we are in a place called Muckle Flugga which is in the Shetland Islands. "If Mr Blair gets in," I told the people queuing to get into Star Wars 3, "this place will no longer be part of England." They all cheered, which shows how wrong the polls are.

Wednesday

The polls have finally got it right. There is one in the Guardian which shows that Mr Blair's lead has totally collapsed. I read about it in the Daily Telegraph and the Daily Mail, when we stopped for a photo-opportunity outside the Happy Eater in a place called Llandudno. When I told the people who were queuing that if Mr Blair gets in, this place would no longer be part of England, they all cheered again. We then drove to Cornwall to unveil Mr Dr Mawhinney's latest poster. I was very shocked to see that it showed Mr Herr Kohl sitting in a chair with Mr Blair on his knee. "Shouldn't that be me?" I said. "After all, I am the one who is Mr Herr Kohl's friend, not Mr Blair." "Shut up, you idiot, prime minister," he said, "this is our new secret weapon, Europe. We are suggesting that Herr Kohl is a paedophile." "I thought he was a Christian Democrat," I said. Mr Dr Mawhinney got very angry, and told everyone to get back in the bus as we had to be in Weymouth by 4.48 for a photo-opportunity in front of Mr Howard's new floating prison. "A grammar school in every prison," I told Norman, "that is my new idea for this afternoon." "Have you been in the toilet with the man from the Observer?" she said suspiciously, examining my arm in a curious manner. "I think you are in need of a long holiday," I told her. "I am about to get one," she said.

Thursday

More good news. Our candidates all over the country are at last right

behind me in my policy on Europe. They have all declared that they are totally against the Single Currency, which is also my own position, except that I am also totally in favour of it. This shows that we are a united party. This is such a welcome display of support that Mr Dr Mawhinney quickly organised a broadcast on all channels for me to make what he called an emergency appeal to the nation. "What shall I say?" I said. "It's alright, prime minister," he assured me. "It'll be completely spontaneous. You just read it off the autocue." This is my historic speech in full. "Good evening (LOOK SINCERE). I am now going to tear up the speech I was going to make (TEAR UP BLANK SHEETS OF PAPER) and speak to you from the heart (PUT HAND ON HEART — THIS IS TO THE LEFT OF YOUR TIE). Who governs Britain? That is the question. Is it me or is it Brussels? (LOOK WORRIED) My message is simple. Back me or I stay. Do not send me naked into the toilet with Mr Self. Good night."

Friday

My historic broadcast has turned the tide at last. Not that the tide needed turning. Oh no. Mr Monsieur Santer has played right into my hands, in no small measure. He has sent an ultimatum saying that, although he has no wish to interfere in a British election, it was the duty of everyone in Britain to vote for Mr Blair. I am incandescent with pleasure, as this shows once and for all that Mr Blair is just a puppet on a string being manipulated by the faceless child

molesters of Brussels. The election has come alive at last, and a new poll shows that I am only three points behind Mr Santer as the most unpopular man in Europe.

Monday

I am totally incandescent with incandescence over Mr Blair saying I am going to do away with the state pension. Let there be no doubt. "The day pensions are abolished", I told my wife Norman, "will be the day I give up politics altogether." "So that will be May 2nd," said Norman.

This is typical. Whilst I have been out on the campaign winning hearts and minds, if not actual votes, she has been ringing up someone called Mr Pickford and asking him for "quotes".

"I am the one who gives quotes round here," I told her, "and today's one is this: Mr Blair is a liar. And his pants are on fire. Oh yes."

Mr Dr Mawhinney has come up with a final brilliant poster saying "Tony is a B.Liar".

This is brilliant although it is a pity that it is mis-spelt and it is too late to change it.

Tuesday

I told Norman to take my Bastard Books out of the tea chest as I had another name to add to the list. It is Mrs Currie who has told the newspapers that the Tories are going to lose and it will all be my fault. How dare she? We are not going to lose and if we were I would not be able to sack her next week, as she would have lost her seat and so would I, which I am not going to do. Oh yes. Or oh no.

Eve of Poll

I have not yet decided which way I am going to vote. As far as voting Conservative is concerned, I would not rule it in or rule it out. We must wait and see what the conditions will be inside the polling booths. This has been a very long campaign and the main thing is that I must not crack up like Mr Blair. Tomorrow I shall vote for the future of Britain and then it is up to the people to decide. If by any chance I were to lose, which I will not, there is no doubt in my mind who is to blame. My brother Terry, who has done so much to undermine my image as a world statesman and to give a totally false idea of my background in Brixton. For example, on page 132 of his book, which I have never read, he says that a consignment of gnomes despatched to Digwell's of Chertsey, Specialists in Garden Ornaments and Horticultural Furniture, was wrongly delivered to a Mr Cyril Squirrel and that this was somehow all my fault...

Editor's Note

At this point the writing in the diary becomes indistinct and then peters out in an illegible blur *(surely Blair? Ed.)*.

ST ALBION PARISH NEWS

The Vicarage

Hello! I'm Tony, your new vicar! And that's what I'd like you to call me — Tony!

The first thing I'd like to do is to give a big thank-you to everybody for choosing me as the new incumbent, and to say what a lovely warm welcome you've given myself and Cherie! I hope you will get to know her as well as me in the challenging years ahead, although she will be continuing with her career as she has every right to do!

It is a truly awesome responsibility you have placed on my shoulders, and I shall do my utmost to be worthy of the trust you have placed in me!

You will not need me to tell you that there is much to do, and that this is a tough parish to take on!

Things have got pretty run-down in recent years, as we all know, and our financial position leaves a good deal to be desired! And that's why we're very fortunate that Mr Brown, the bank manager, has agreed to

come in and do the books!

As you know, Cherie and I have just moved into the vicarage, which was clearly not designed for a young family with high-spirited children!

Still, all is going well, and there is even room for my guitar, which those of you who come to evensong will soon be hearing more of! You have been warned!

I know what a lot of you are wondering is — are there going to be any changes in the way St Albion's is run?

The answer is, yes and no! Yes there are, and no there aren't! But

more of that later! But the main thing is that I intend to hit the ground running!

I've got a great team of helpers, especially a huge number of ladies (I'm not complaining about that!) and I know that we're all singing from the same hymn sheet (Mr Mandelson, our new churchwarden, is going to make sure of that!).

I will leave you this time with just one thought. Being in charge here means that I and my team think of ourselves as very much the servants and not the masters! And don't let's forget that we're here to serve the *whole* community. That means everyone, not just the Faithful!

See you on Sunday!

Tony

PS. I don't know who started the rumours about the vicarage cat, Humphrey, but let me assure you he's still very much part of the team!

Notices

House Groups will meet as usual on Wednesday (Mrs Mortimer), Thursday (Mrs Harris) and Saturday (Lady Powell).

On Friday Mrs Follett will talk on "What Our Clothes Say About Us", 8pm Church Hall. (Everyone must be there! P.M.)

The Week Ahead

Monday. Join Social Chapter (Mr Cook in charge).

Tuesday. Ms Mowlam opens the Mission to Northern Ireland at St Gerry's.

Wednesday. There will be a full meeting of the new PCC in Church House for an address by the Vicar, supported by Mr Prescott from the Working Men's Club.

Thursday. Ms Short will be launching her new outreach programme for the Third World.

N.B. If you want to see the vicar and ask him any questions, he is available at any time, i.e. Wednesdays between 3.00 and 3.30. (*I know this marks a change from my predecessor's practice but I think you'll see this gives us all more time to have a proper chat! Tony.*)

Our New Vicar

by Mr Mandelson

No one is more pleased than I am that we've finally got Tony installed as our new incumbent. I don't mind saying that it is entirely thanks to me that he is where he is today. The main thing now is that we all work as a team, and if anyone's got any problems, they come and talk to me first. We don't want any of the sort of unpleasantness that this parish has had in the recent past! Believe you me, there are plenty of people out there who are only too ready

to knock us for our beliefs, whatever they are. So, it is very important that no one does anything until the PCC (that's me basically!) gives them the go-ahead. I want you all to remember that!

P.M.

A Spring Morning

Verses by a local poet

The long darkness is over!
The winter of fascism is at an end!
Thank God (if he exists)!
The cherry trees are pink with blossom!
Birds are singing!
The sun shines!
Hats off to Tony!

H. Pinter (93)

The Parish Newsletter is edited by Alistair Campbell. No outside contributions welcome.

GOLDILOCKS AND THE THREE BLAIRS

NEW LABOUR

New Labour — New Glenda ✱ ✱ ✱ ✱ ✱ *The Gal Who Is Hitting The Sack Running (Geddit!?!)* ✱ ✱ ✱ ✱ ✱ ✱ ✱

GLENDA SLAGG

CHERIE Blair — Aren'tchasickofher! If I see one more shot of **Cherie a-grinnin' and a-gawpin'** like some gargoyle that's fallen off the church roof I think I'll throw up!?! Go on, clear off Cherie!? Get back to your courtroom and leave the rest of us to enjoy breakfast in peace!?!

CHERIE Blair — Don'tchaluvher?! A working mother who knows how to stand by her man as well?!! With her sexy wig and expensive briefs (geddit?!!) she's a shining example to every gal in town of how a modern missus can have it all?!! I judge this Juicy QC to be the best First Lady we've ever had!?!! (Geddit!?) All stand!?!!

HATS off to David Helfgott!?! — Mr Shine, stoopid!?! OK, so he's bonkers and can't play the piano! Who cares!? I'd rather watch dishy David a-mutterin' and a-splutterin', a-hummin' and a-strummin', a-twinklin' and a-tinklin' (Get on with it. Ed.) over the Rachmaninov than some bow-tied bore in a dinner jacket any day!?! Mmm!?! Shine on me, mister, you ain't helf gott what it takes!? Geddit!?!!

SEEN the English Patient yet?! Z-z-z-z-z-!?!! Put me out of my misery, doctor, and give us the morphine!?!!

HERE they are, Glenda's own Blair Babes!?!

● **Frank Dobson** — the new Health Minister!? With his bushy beard and roly-poly eyes, there'll be no waiting list for my bed?! Geddit?!

● **Dr Jack Cunningham** — M-m-m-minister for Agriculture!? OK, so he's been sidelined, but here's one mad cow who still thinks he's sexy!!?!!

● **Lord Irvine of Lairg!** Crazee name, crazee appointment *(surely 'guy'? Ed.)*

Byeeee!!!

Cat Under Threat

That New Labour Ministers' Briefing Lunch in full

No One in the Soup (Campbells)

— ✱ —

No Egg on Face

— ✱ —

No Beef with No Leaks and Unspilt Beans

— ✱ —

 Hard Cheese

— ✱ —

To drink:
Nothing

66

IT'S BACK!

NEW LABOUR, NEW HANZ-Z-Z-ARD

New Prime Minister's Question Time. 3 p.m.

Ms Renata Anglepoise (Tunbridge Wells, New Lab): May I just ask Tony, I mean the Prime Minister *(Labour cheers)* how it feels to have won such a brilliant victory in the recent election, and does he agree that, from now on, things can only get better?

Mr A. Blair (Sedgemore, New Lab): I would like to thank the Member for Tunbridge Wells for her acute analysis of recent events and to thank her for being one of the many thousands of new women MPs who will, I am sure, bring a wholly new, civilised tone to our proceedings in this House. *(Thousands of New Labour women MPs scream "Tony! Tony!" and ask for his autograph)*

Dame Boothroyd *(for it is still she):* Order! Order! Remember where you are. Please remember the dignity of this House!

Ms Patsy Jacket (Billericay, New Lab): Can I ask the Prime Minister whether he would agree that the use of landmines is totally unacceptable to a civilised society?

Mr A. Blair (Sedgefield, New Lab): I'm glad you were told to ask me that question, Patsy. Now that you mention it, I do happen to have here a ten-point plan for the total ban of all landmines, except, obviously, all the ones the Chinese make. *(Prime Minister reads out long statement lasting for most of the available parliamentary time)*

Ms Stephanie Twigg (Portillo East, New Lab): Can I ask why there isn't a proper unisex hairdresser in this place? All we've got is a sexist male chauvinist barber who had the nerve to ask me whether I wanted something for the weekend.

Mr Alan Clark (Kensington and Legovia, Con): I'll give you something for the weekend, darling! *(Tory cheers and cries of "Clarkie for leader!")*

Mr Dennis Bolsover (Skinner, Lab): What I would like to ask this so-called Labour Prime Minister is why the first thing he does is to grovel to the capitalists and bankers by privatising the Bank of England to fat-cat gnomes in Zurich like Eddie George? *(Labour cries of "Oh really!" "Grow up, Dennis!" "We're not living in the Middle Ages!")*

Mr A. Blair: I don't think under our new rules that I have to answer that question! *(Labour cheers. Entire backbenches begin singing "Things can only get getter")*

Dame Boothroyd: Order! Order! Wouldn't any of the Tories like to ask a question? Come on, come on! I'm sure some of you have got something to ask Mr Blair. He won't bite you!

Mr J. Vulcan (Redwood, Con): Would the Prime Minister agree that Mr Clarke and Mr Hague and Mr Howard are utterly useless and spineless and would be really hopeless as leader of the Conservative Party, and would he also further agree that there is only one sensible candidate for that office who is capable of re-uniting the party round a policy of taking us out of Europe and onto Mars? *(Tories all start fighting amongst themselves)*

Mr P. Ashtray (Pantsdown Lib Dem): Could I remind the Prime Minister that my party is now bigger than ever… pivotal role… proportional representation… penny on income tax… hung parliament… *(House empties)*

© New Hanz-z-z-ard: "Things Can Only Get More Boring".

JOBSEEKERS

Crème de la Brûlée

AN EYE SERVICE

Spanish-speaker, 45, with Cambridge degree, some experience public speaking, has appeared on TV, seeks full-time employment, possibly in defence industry. Anything considered. Box: Xavier 1.

Spywriter, 33, desperately seeks someone to sue after unfortunate reversal of fortune. Wife, blonde violinist and four houses to support. Box: Gonewest 6.

Brother of former Prime Minister, 57, well-known author and newspaper columnist, with own mobile phone, finds himself unexpectedly available for night-club evenings, garden ornament conventions etc. Box: Terry 3

Self-publicist and best-selling author ("dirty bits a speciality"), 55, with experience of eggs, very keen on Europe, finds herself unjustifiably in search of work due to the spineless incompetence of everyone except herself. Will do absolutely anything to keep name in papers. Box: Eggwina 999.

The Lady Olga Maitland wishes it to be known that she is now considering a career move, due to a recent unforeseen change in her circumstances. Send generously please to Distressed Elderly Gentlefolk's Association, Sutton and Cheam. Box: Olgmait 4.

Duplicitous Old Etonian, brother of Earl, will consider any directorships over £250,000. Experience of arms sales, official enquiries and fish. Also available for functions as butler, with wife doubling as cook. Box: Wargrave 5.

Edinburgh-born lawyer, 51, with experience in foreign affairs, now available to do his famous Dalek impersonation at children's parties. Box: Rifkind 7.

200 more appear on pages 94-206.

Cat Reprieved

I'm going to hit the mouse running

Nine out of Number Ten owners prefer publicity

Introducing Britain's Newest Fanzine

BLAIRZONE

Everything you need to know about Britain's most popular Band

Message from Tony (lead singer of Blairzone)

HEY! Wow! This is some gig, eh? But I couldn't have got where I am without you — the fans! No, really. But as the late, great Freddy Mercury put it, "We are the champions, my friends, and we'll go on fighting till the end".

And just 'cos we're top of the hit parade doesn't mean we're going to sit back and take it easy! As the late great Harry Nilsson said, "Gotta get up, gotta get up" on the B side of "Can't live if living is without you". Right on Harry.

And hey listen — me and the band are going to put together a totally new sound. Not so new that you don't like it but more a sort of classical progressive rock fusion sound — like Barclay James Harvest's "Galadriel" — remember that? Rock and roll!!

Love ya,
Tony.

Tony Fax File

❶ Tony has 200 pairs of shoes.

❷ When on tour Tony likes to chill out with the roadies and crack open a bottle of Veuve Cliquot 1993!!

❸ Tony's top influences are Guns 'n' Roses, Led Zep, Showaddywaddy and Archbishop William Temple's Christianity and the Social Order!!

❹ Tony's guitar is a Stratosfender 74 with double slide wah-wah handle. He also owns a recorder and a xylophone!?!

❺ Tony's favourite colour is (Deep) Purple.

Tony Thinx!

Tony and the boys from Blairzone are not just pretty faces (though they are, girls!!) — they've got a whole philosophy of life, which Tony describes as "Walkin' on Sunshine" in the words of the late, great Katrina and the Waves.

Tony Lixe

Babes
Flares
An Independent Bank of England

Tony Dislixe

Drugs
Hip-Hop
Ministers having briefing lunches with journalists

Groupie Heaven (or as the late great band Sailor put it, "Girls, girls, girls"!!)

From The Referendum Bunker

No 94: A Final Bulletin To My Millions Of Followers

Achtung!

So. Everybody. You think you have seen the last of me.

But I tell you. We were not defeated.

We were betrayed. By the people of Britain. Who were stupid enough to give their votes to everyone but me.

And the media were just as bad. They all betrayed me too. All of them.

Except of course my loyal henchman Taki.

He alone courageously supported my cause to the end. Which is probably why we lost.

(Presses button which throws swarthy Greek tennis player into huge vat of boiling Marmite filled with killer whitebait — the property of the J. Aspinall Whitebait Experience, Margate)

And now, my dear Carla, we are alone.

(Turns round to find that ageing, mini-skirted temptress has defected to New Labour, leaving note:)

Darling Jimmy,
It was a great party but it's all over. Now I have found a better one and my heart belongs to Peter. I have gone off to our victory celebrations at the Festival Hall. Don't be angry, Jimmy. Che sera, sera.

Yours unfaithfully,
Carla Power-Mad.

(Sir Jammy strokes white powder in capsule)

I have here a cyanide pill. I am sure all of you expect me to swallow it. But you are wrong Mr Bond, Mr Major, Mr Blair, Mr Ashdown, Mr Middle England.

You are fools, all of you. Do you hear me?

I am not finished. Not by a long way. One day I will be back. And in the meantime I shall be watching you from my secret hideaway on the comet Hale-Bopp.

Goodbye. Or should I say Auf Wiedersehen Schweinhunden.

(Climbs into Tardis and disappears into cyber-reality to sound of Theme from Silence of the Jams)

"Of course it's crap, sir — you said everything had to go through Mr Mandelson first"

— Geoff Thompson —

Lives of the Saints

St Martin slays the dragon (Paulo Ucello)

No. 94: St Martin of Bell

IN THE last days of King John the Useless, the land of Albion was struck by a great plague of sleaze. Everywhere was infected and the people knew not whither to turn. And, worst of all, a mighty dragon appeared in the forests of Tatton, dragging behind her an obedient slave called Neil. And the people cried "Who will save us?" But no one came forward, no not one. Then finally there stepped out a knight in shining white linen, who was called Martin. "Good folk," he said. "I have heard of your plight even in the distant land of Bosnia. And I have come to rescue you in your hour of distress." And he showed the people his wounds and his beautiful daughter. And they were overjoyed. Then Martin sallied forth to face the dragon, completely unarmed. And the dragon scorched him with her fire. And Martin said nothing, but sent his white suit to the cleaners. And when it was returned he sallied forth again, armed this time with some old cuttings from the Grauniad.

The votes were cast as follows:

Hamilton, N. (Conservative) 2
Hamilton, C. (Dragon) 10,412
Bell, M. (Anti-Sleaze and Dragonslaying Alliance) 32,841

The returning officer duly recorded that Mr Bell was elected to serve as a saint for the next five years. And from that day forth he took a vow of silence, for he had nothing further to say.

**NEXT WEEK:
St Mo of Mowlam.**

The bad old days

Children's Corner

New Labour Guide To The New Britain

No. 94: Trade Unions

A TRADE union is a body which has nothing whatever to do with the Labour Government. In the bad old days workers ganged up on bosses to demand silly things like a living wage and better living conditions.

Once they got what they wanted the union bosses became the most powerful people in the land. They wore top hats and drank champagne, while the poor bosses starved to death in the streets. But luckily all that changed when Tony Blair became leader of the New Labour Party. The trade unions were put firmly in their place, the bosses were all given jobs in the government and everyone lived happily ever after.

Typical Trade Unions include the CBI, the IoD and the Civil Service First Division.

Lives of the Saints

No. 94: St Ann of Widdecombe

AND IN those times there lived a pious virgin whose name was Ann. And Ann took no care of her person, believing all paints and other self-adornment to be but empty vanities. This holy maiden devoted her days to the welfare of prisoners, building more and more prisons to house them and providing much-needed shackles for those female prisoners who were in labour.

But, after many years working in this wise, Ann encountered the devil himself, incarnated as a petty ruler set over her — by name the Lord Howard. For a time she held her peace, meekly accepting all the tasks which Howard laid upon her. But the day came when Howard sought to rise yet higher, and to become one of the most powerful men in the kingdom. Then God appeared to Ann in a vision and said unto her: "Now is thy chance. Put

thy boot in and really stitch him up. Go on, thou knowest thou will enjoy it."

And the blessed Ann spent many hours in prayer and fasting, meditating on how she might best carry out the Divine Will and drive the foul fiend from out of the land. And, behold, there came to her in her cell a clerk from the Anglo-Saxon Telegraph (edited by the Venerable Charles Moore). And Ann cried out: "There is something of the night about Master Howard."

And when he read this, the Lord Howard went pale and began to quake, even unto his boots. And with a demonic shriek of "Lo! I am undone!", the fiend vanished in a puff of sulphurous smoke and was seen no more in the land. And from that day forth, Ann was renowned for her powers of exorcism and was held by all to be a saint.

NEXT WEEK: Swampy, the Holy Hermit of Manchester.

JERRY PREGNANT SHOCK

I'm having this one without any drugs

Speak for yourself

GLENDA SLAGG

The One-Woman Spice Girls!?!!

MAGGIE'S back!?? Well excooose me, mister!?! I thought we'd seen the last of that old crone when she climbed on her broomstick and flew into the sunset!?! *(shurely 'Moonshine'? Ed.)* Now we see so-called New Labour Blair a-crawlin' and a-fawnin' to Mystic Mag in the hope of getting some answers from her crystal balls!?!! Here's one prediction from Madame Glenda: stick with Maggie mate and you can kiss Downing Street goodbye!?!!

HATS off to Tony Blair!? At last a Labour leader has had the guts to talk to the one person in the country that everyone admires!? There he was going round to her house, cloth cap in hand, asking: "Maggie! Maggie! Maggie! What on earth do I do now?".

OK, so she may be old and mad, but this geriatric granny has got more wisdom in her little finger than all the jumped up schoolboys in the cabinet put together!? Three cheers for the new double act — Tony and Maggie!?!

HELEN Mirren — Aren'tchasick-ofher? Prime Suspect? Past-Your-Prime I suspect!? (Geddit?!!) So some magazine reckons you're the world's sexiest woman!?! What is it?! The magazine of the Royal National Institute of the Blind?!! Clear off DCI Tennison so called and put yourself away for a long time!?!

HELEN Mirren — what a star!? 51 years old and you would never know it?! Svelte, sexy and simply super!?! No wonder the public have acclaimed her the most beautiful woman since Cleopatra!?! If I look like that when I'm 51 I shall die a happy woman!?! *(Who are you trying to kid? Ed.)*

SEEN Teletubbies?! Me neither!!

HERE they are Glenda's Chelsea Floor Show!?

● **Lord Chadlington** — he's the sexy supremo of the Royal Opera House! And he's Selwyn Gummer's brother?! What more could any gal want?

● **R.B. Kitaj** — The World's greatest painter is quitting Britain for ever?! Pleazze reconsider Mr K? I do a bit of nude modelling and I might get my Kitaj off for you — Geddit!?!

● **Mohammed Sarwar** — Crazy name, crazy bribe! *(surely 'Guy' Ed?)*

Byeeee!

I THINK YOU'LL FIND THE GREAT REFORM ACT WAS *MAY* NOT MARCH 1832

Teddy Bears Nit Pick

THE LORD'S DAYLY TELEGRAPH

Outrage As 'Plotters' Enter Parliament

by Our Political Staff Boris Johnfon

Guido Fawkes   Robert Catefby

YE MOTHER of Parliaments was in uproar yefterday as Mafter Fawkes and Mafter Catefby paid a visit to the House of Commons.

Ye two reprefentatives of the Gunpowder community dined heartily at ye agreeable subfidifed buffet before attempting to take a guided tour of ye famous cellars. Mefsrs Fawkes and Catefby were however barred from taking ye part in any of ye proceedings of His Majefty's Parliament.

"This is exceeding irkfome," saith Master Fawkes. "Ye only thinge we are defirous of doing is to enter ye Parliament and blow it up. What is ye problem with that?"

ON OTHER PAGES

How They Are Related (or not)

Hughie Green

Sir Hugh Carlton-Green
|
Sir Hughie Green
|
Hughie Grant
|
Huey
|
Dewey
|
Louie
|
Louis Armstrong-Jones

Paula Yates

W.B. Yeats
|
Jess Yates
|
Helene Bosman
|
Helen Bosman-Carter
|
Noel Botham-Carter
|
Ian Botham
|
Paul McCartney

Louis Armstrong-Jones —— *m.* —— Paul McCartney
|
Paul Yates

Ein Deutschmark (or 3 million Euros)

Der Kindergarten Telegraaf

(incorporating Mother Goosestep's Nursery Rhymes)

SETBACK FOR KING KOHL'S MASTERPLAN

Gold 'fiddlers' exposed

by Our Man in Bonn **Tony Bundesbanks**

OLD King Kohl was distinctly unmerry yesterday, when he was caught out in a scam involving his so-called "fiddlers three".

The King had called on his fiddlers to go in the middle of the night to his counting house, and report on how much gold was stored in the vaults.

They were then ordered to multiply the value of the gold by ten, in order to meet Maastricht convergence criteria.

This was a key move in his plan to take over the whole of Europe.

Mass Tricked

The scam was exposed when a small boy, little Hans Tietmayer, saw what was going on and shouted out: "Look, Emperor Kohl hasn't got any gold after all!"

The King then got into a tremendous bate and said that his plans for economic and monetary union would continue anyway.

Old King Kohl is 107.

CRICKET MAN DEAD

by the late **Sir Denis Compton**

TO EVERY schoolboy who lived through the colourful eighties and nineties John Major was an extraordinary flash of dullness — a taste of grey in a world of technicolour life and gaiety.

With his trademark glasses and slicked-forward hair Major became known as the "Grecian 2000 Boy" and cut a figure of exceptional boredom on and off the field. He soon became one of the least loved personalities in the game.

Flannel

Those who saw his innings at the dispatch box in the summer of '97 could never remember a word he said. In a number of spectacularly bad performances for England he made hundreds of speeches, effortlessly deflecting questions with a flick of his ringbinder, and sending the spectators into a frenzy of sleep.

All Out

No more will we see him despatching balls into the crowd. No more will we see him putting on his soapbox and being hit by his opponent's delivery. No more of this piece thank you very much. Ed.

The Feelgood Factor

Ten tell-tale signs that it's really happening!

1. Summer is here!
2. It's raining!
3. The Halifax are giving us all money!
4. Mike Atherton's boys are doing us proud!
5. Glen Hoddle's lads are doing us prouder!
6. Jewel In The Crown is back on TV!
7. The Spice Girls are showing their knickers on the front page of the Telegraph!
8. Only six months 'til Christmas!
9. Noel from Oasis has got married!
10. Punch is about to fold!

Let us know what makes you feel good!
Just e-mail Will Hutton (The Observer's Mr Happy)
at statewerein@absurder.rubbish.co.uk
or phone 0898 742378 (it's much quicker).

Life before Estate Agents

BRITAIN'S NO. 1 SPORTING EVENT

The F.A. Cup Final 1997

Chelsea v. Middlesbrough

MIDDLESBROUGH

Mobutu

Ceaucescu Guantanamera Ikea Oranjeboom

Van der Post Vorsprung Durch Technik

Portillo

Canelloni

Palestrina Shostakovich

Schnittke Björk Altarica Ipanema Zapata

De Kooning Kalahsnikov Balzac

Kebila

CHELSEA

MIDDLESBROUGH – Manager: Jacques Delors
CHELSEA – Manager: Hugh Montgomery-Massingberd
(shurely shome mishtake? Ed)

Wembley – For the Best in English Football!

Semen Behaving Badly

GLENDA SLAGG

Hitting you for sex!!?!
(surely 'six'? Ed)

KENNETH Clarke — don'tcha-luvhim!?! OK. So he's fat and fifty-seven, but at least he's human!?! With his filthy shoes from Oxfam and his tie that smells of beer, cuddly Ken is the Roly-Poly Romeo who can put the "it" back into "politics"!? Get it? I wish I did from Ken?! No offence Mrs Clarke but you shouldn't have married a sex bomb?!

KENNETH Clarke! 'oo'd vote for him?! Not me mister!? With his beer gut, stinking panatella and curry-stained trousers, I say this yesterday's man should be put in a bottle bank!? Take a tip from Auntie Glenda, Ken – crawl back into the pub and stop blowing your trumpet!? You're just a jazz-been!? Geddit!? I don't unfortunately but I wouldn't mind if it was pouting Peter Lilley!? I always liked the strong silent type!? Sorry Mrs Lilley but you shouldn't have married a professional love-machine!?!

HERE they are — Glenda's Testosterone Team!?!

● **M-m-m-Michael Atherton**!?! I wouldn't mind tampering with his ball (geddit?!!)

● **M-m-m-Mark Taylor**!?! He can stroke this maiden through the covers any day or night!? (Geddit?!!)

● **Greg Blewett**!?! *(This bit has been censored. Ed.)*

● **M-m-m-Michael Kasprowicz**!?! Crazy name, crazy medium-pace guy!?!

Leg-Byeeee!?!

ENGLAND GO BACK TO BASICS

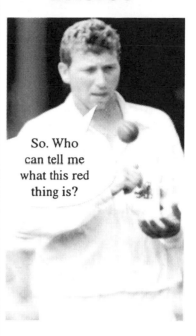

So. Who can tell me what this red thing is?

"The Englishman goes to the beach once a year to shed his skin…"

— PILBROW —

Peter McLie

The World's Worst Columnist

☐ THE Conservative Party are looking, I hear, for a new leader. I have a suggestion: step forward John Major. This young man would be a breath of fresh air to a tired and jaded party! And no one can say he lacks experience. Go on, vote for John. I'm sure the country will next time round.

☐ THE cricket season seems to go on longer and longer every year — here we are in flamin' June and they are still at it. Why can't we have a new game to play in the summer? Why not, for example, two sides of eleven men chasing a round leather ball which they have to kick into a net suspended by white posts?! I even have a name for such a sport: Association Trouser Press. *(You're fired. Ed.)*

Notes & Queries

QUESTION: How did "the Ashes" get their name? — *E.B. Bail, Somerset.*

☐ THE famous Ashes are named after the Glamorgan and England cricketer Cyril Ashes who with his brother Lionel (L.B. Ashes) first proposed a tournament between England and South Africa in 1899. When the South Africans failed to raise a team during the Boer War the invitation was extended to the Pakistanis instead. It has taken place every year ever since. — *Professor D. Trelford, Department of Media Studies, Sheffield.*

QUESTION: Can bats swim? — *Mrs Enid Rusbridger, Preston.*

☐ C.J.P. Barkworth is wrong to state (N&Q, 29 Feb) that there is one species of bat which is amphibious. The bat he refers to, Pippistrella Nautilus Normalis, the so-called "swimming bat of Papua New Guinea" is not a bat at all and was wrongly classified as such by the Rev J.D. Googly in "Bats of Papua New Guinea" (1899). This animal is in fact a member of the newt family which sleeps upside down and is the only newt capable of flight. —

Dr David Bergasol MRDF, Editor "Bats and Batmen".

QUESTION: What is Will Self's real name? — *Ved Frobisher, Lahore University.*

☐ THE man who calls himself Will Self was born The Hon. Archibald Massingberd-Montgomery-Smythe. His father, Sir Hugo, was Equerry to King George VI (1948-1953) and his mother Lady Laetitia (née von Bösendorfer-Steinway) was a renowned horsewoman and socialite. It was at Eton that Archibald first assumed the name Wilf Self as a pseudonym for obscene short stories he submitted to the Eton Chronicle. They were never used but Archibald kept the name, adapting it only slightly by deed poll to Will Self in 1977 when he went to read Land Economy at Christ Church College, Oxford. — *Lady Elizabeth Calder, Publisher of Bloomsbury Books.*

NEXT WEEK: Answers to the following please: Has anyone ever been born with two left feet? Is Domestos the smallest Greek island? Who first discovered rhubarb? What is the difference between Anne McIlroy and Anne Applebaum? *(That's enough queries. Ed.)*

I-SPY

NOTORIOUS BLAIR STREET →

Silverton, Colorado

STRICTLY NO PARKING IN THIS CAR PARK

The Maltings, Ely

SANDRA 50 m ←

Prague

CHIROPODIST 3 O.FEET ☜

Newquay, Cornwall

NESSUN DORMA BED & BREAKFAST
FACILITIES IN ALL ROOMS

Plockton, Wester Ross, Scotland

MICHAEL PINTO (GOVT. LICENCE) FUNERAL DIRECTORS SCULPTORS AND EMBALMERS
WHEN YOU DROP DEAD DROP IN
4308569 4373958

Bombay

KINKI NIPPON TOURIST CO., LTD.

Vienna

IF YOU ♥ HAWAII BONK MAYOR

Hawaii

TAKI FRIED CHICKEN →

Rabat, Morocco

Coca-Cola WANKIE MEAT SUPPLIES

Zimbabwe

Ayrshire

M&B COTTAGE SPRING M&B
BRITAIN IS BOOMING. DON'T LET LABOUR BLOW IT.

Tipton, W. Midlands

BLAIR POLICIES
Open for pedestrians only 9am-8pm
No cars, bicycles or dogs
Please keep to paths and do not leave any litter or disturb flowers or trees

Keighley, W. Yorkshire

Blarney, Ireland

Settle, N. Yorkshire

Douglas, Isle of Man

GOAD & BUTCHER SOLICITORS

Florida

MAJORS CREEK

NSW, Australia

Secret Bunker

Amsterdam

Long Stratton

funeral centre
the last ones to let you down

Harare, Zimbabwe

LUDLOW FESTIVAL
MUCH ADO ABOUT
NOTHING
June 21st - July 5th

IN THE COURTS

Before Mr Justice Popplecarrot
The case of Aitken v. Grauniad Newspapers and Graunada TV

Mr Charles Grayman Q.C. (*for the plaintiff*): My lord, I move first of all that this very important and complex case, involving as it does more than 20,000 witnesses, 200,000 documents and £2,000,000 payable to myself, is not one which is best determined by a jury, consisting, you may think, of some dozen persons of either sex, dragged in off the street, many of them illiterate, unwashed and of uncertain ethnic origin. Furthermore, my lord, many of these pitiful creatures, I submit, may be silly, scatterbrained women of the female kind, who would be better served staying at home with their illegitimate children, watching Kilroy.

Mr Justice Popplecarrot (*waking up*): What is Kilroy?

(*Laughter in court*)

Mr Carperson (*for the defendants*): M'lud, may I try to ingratiate myself with you at this point by explaining to your lordship that Kilroy is a television programme, taking its name from a Mr Kilroy-Silk.

Judge: Is he a silk, Mr Carperson?

(*Counsel collapse in hysterical laughter*)

Mr Grayman: If I may return, my lord, to the *gravamen* of the *res materia* in this case, my submission is that there is only one person in the entire kingdom, not to say universe, endowed with the necessary powers of perspicacity, wisdom (*asks junior to hand over copy of Roget's Thesaurus*), ah yes, intelligence, mental agility, crocodile tears… I beg your pardon, my lord, I was reading from the wrong bundle.

Judge: So it would appear, Mr Grayman. But you were about to say that only I was suitable to hear this case as a *solex adjudicatus*?

Krayman: If it so pleaseth, your lordship.

Judge: So be it. Send the jury home, to continue watching Mr Killjoy, and we lawyers will sort this one between us *sine pleibianibus*.

(*All lawyers laugh at thought of working classes*)

Grayman: I am indebted to your lordship. May I now proceed to my opening submissions? In this case I have the honour to represent one of the most outstanding public servants of this or indeed any other age, Mr Jeffrey Archer. (*Junior tugs gown and whispered consultation takes place*) Oh yes, my Junior Mr Fearnley-Whittingstall, has corrected me on a point of law. My client is in fact Mr Jonathan Aitken, the former Chief Secretary to the Treasury and Women Procurement minister.

(*Junior tugs gown again*)

My lord, I meant of course Defence Procurement. My client is not only a statesman of world renown, he is also a highly respected member of the international business community, a director *inter alios* of such companies as Roland Rat Television Productions Ltd, the Saudi Scientific Instrumentation Design Co, Anglo-Indonesian Security Services (Singapore) Ltd, the Arabian Cultural Exchange, Frith Street, Soho, the Inglenooky Sauna and Massage Advisory Centre, Kinkbury, Berks, the Arms R Us Peace Foundation (Riyadh) and many other enterprises too numerous to register.

Judge: He is obviously innocent.

Mr Carperson: My lord, I think it might be a little premature to end the case at this juncture. There is a good deal more evidence to be offered before we all send in our bills!

Judge: A good point, Mr Carperson. Pray proceed, Mr Grayman.

Graystoke: My client, Mr Aitken has been subjected by the defendants, I submit, to the vilest and most opprobrious campaign of vilification that I have ever witnessed in my long carer at the Bar.

Judge: You always say that Mr Grayman, ha, ha, ha.

Grayman: I am indebted to your lordship. Nevertheless, you catch my drift. As a result of this malicious and odious farrago of lies and baseless calumnies, my client's reputation has been butchered, his distinguished political career brought crashing in ruins, his marriage in tatters after his admission of adultery. (*Junior tugs gown again*) I'm sorry, my lord, could the jury, if we had one, strike that one from their memories? But to sum up, I would submit that my client has suffered every indignity known to mankind, including most lately, his rejection by the electors of Thanet East, all directly attributable to the evil campaign of bullying and mendacity systematically mounted against him by the media conglomerates run by Mr Alan Rubbisher, whom you see skulking behind my learned friend like one of Mr Tesco's frozen chickens.

Judge: My clerk informs me that an interesting situation has arisen in the Test Match, and I would therefore suggest that this is a suitable moment to adjourn.

The Court rose at 94-8.
The case continues.

A Taxi-Driver writes

EVERY week a well-known taxi driver is invited to give his opinion on an issue of topical importance.

This week: Paul Johnson (Cab No.982) writes on the collapse of the Jonathan Aitken libel action.

Blimey, guv! I don't see what all the fuss is about meself! I mean, 'e's workin' for the government right so 'e's got to lie, inne, or he'll be found out? Stands to reason — and 'e's gotta sell 'em arms cos that's his job. And if that means layin' on a couple of jam tarts for the Arabs then good luck to him!

I mean look what's 'appened to 'im now. 'is wife's left him, 'e's lost his job and all 'is money — I think the papers should be ashamed of themselves what they done to 'im and 'is family. They should be taken to court!

All 'e's ever done is help this country back on its feet. I think they should give 'im a medal.

I 'ad that Prince Mohammed in the back of the cab once — I took 'im to Heathrow and charged him £5,000. What's wrong with that?

NEXT WEEK: Taki (Cab No.173) argues that Jonathan Aitken is as innocent as he is.

NEW LABOUR, NEW HANZ-Z-Z-ARD

New Prime Minister's Question Time. 3.00 pm

Ms Janet Cardigan (Bournemouth Central, New Lab): May I congratulate the Prime Minister, I mean, Tony, on his first month in office, when he has already transformed Britain into a better place, where things can only get better? *(New Labour backbenchers perform Mexican wave)*

Mr Tony Blair (Sedgemore, New Lab): I don't think I need to reply to that one! *(Laughter)* But thank you, Janet, all the same.

Ms Jenny Swipecard (Haywards Heath, New Lab): I am sure I am speaking for all the New Women in New Britain when I salute the Prime Minister's brilliant appointment of Ms Harriet Harperson as Britain's first genuine Minister for Women. Would Tony not agree that under the Tories no woman would have been given such a senior job in a million years? *(Tory cries of "Maggie! Maggie! Maggie! Back! Back! Back!")*

Mr Alan Clark (Kensington and Legovia, Old Con): More women the better, I say. *(Tory cheers and cries of "We've got the wrong Clarke for leader")*

Mr Blair: I refer my honourable friend to all the answers I have given previously.

Ms Stephanie Twiglet (Portillo South, New Lab): May I take this opportunity while the House is asleep to congratulate the Prime Minister on the speed with which his Government is acting to clamp down on the scandal of all these cyclists who do not fit bells on their bikes, thus putting toddlers and the elderly seriously at risk on Britain's pedestrianised cycleways?

Mr Blair: Thank you, Stephanie, for asking that question you were told to ask, and I would just like to say that we are bringing forward as a matter of the highest priority legislation not only to make the wearing of seat belts compulsory on bikes, but also to ban the use of mobile phones by rollerbladers. *(Labour cheers)*

Ms Patsy Jacket (Billericay, New Lab): While we're on the subject of banning things, could I ask the Prime Minister whether we could have some new safety regulations on the use of shopping trolleys in supermarket aisles. Only last week in my constituency I was involved in what could have been a very nasty incident in our local Tesco, when a three-trolley collision occurred, and a small toddler was ejected into the exotic fruits and could well have been injured by the kumquats falling on his head. Had it not been for the prompt action of members of the staff, this young child could have been seriously injured instead of just, as it was, receiving nasty stains of kumquat juice all over his trainers.

Mr Dennis Bolsover (Skinner, Old Lab): I've never heard such daft rubbish in all my life. Bring back Maggie.

Dame Betty Boop (New Speaker): Order! Order! Can we get on with some proper old-fashioned questions, please. The man in the front row with the glasses and the grey suit. Yes you!

Mr John Failure (Major, Old Con): What I want to know is why the Prime Minister promised to publish a Bill on Scottish Devolution before introducing a Bill to hold a referendum and yet he is now proposing to introduce the Referendum Bill without publishing the other Bill to which I referred earlier? *(Embarrassed silence as members on both sides of the House try to remember who this figure is)*

Mr Major: Alright, I'll get my coat.

Mr Paddy Ashtray (Pantsdown, Old Dem Libs): As the leader of the third largest party in the history of the universe, may I remind the Prime Minister that my party cannot be ignored… *(All MPs rush to exit doors)*

© New Han-z-z-z-ard

Ping… then Pong… Yes, that's awfully good… the whole ping-pong thingie really works

"One day, son, all this will still be mine"

WE'VE BEEN TOLD BY THE BBC TO USE MORE TRADITIONAL SPEECH

WHY?

BECAUSE WE'VE RECEIVED A MEMO FROM JOHN BIRT

WHAT DOES IT SAY?

IN WHAT IS ABOUT TO HAPPEN OR BECOME THAT WILL HEREAFTER BE APPLIED TO A PURPOSE EXISTING IN GREATER OR ADDITIONAL QUANTITY BELONGING OR RELATING EXCLUSIVELY OR DISTINCTLY BASED ON OR OBTAINED BY TRADITION WHILE ENGAGED IN THE FACULTY OF SPEAKING…

FROM THE HOUSE OF GNOME

*Beautiful Commemorative Mug Offer
To Mark The Historic Wedding In The Crypt
of the House of Commons of the*
<u>Rt Hon William Squitt,</u>
*the Leader of the Conservative Party
and his lovely Welsh bride-to-be*
<u>Miss Ffioncée Jenkins</u>

THIS unique hand-made-style bone china drinking mug has been commissioned by the House of Gnome from the universally-acclaimed ceramic portraitist Sir Ralph Stodswell in a limited edition of only 6 million.

Each mug will be personally signed in facsimile by the bride and groom in the wedding of the century.

This unique souvenir of the most important event in our island history is a work of art which in generations to come will be ranked alongside the Wilton Diptych, Nicholas Hilliard's miniature of the Earl of Essex and the famed Book of Kells.

To secure your own personal stake in Britain's proud heritage, just send £412.99 (plus VAT) to:

Hague Smug Offer, Unit 4, Yeovil Trading Estate, Ashdown, Dorset. (Credit cards welcome)

*Mugs made in People's Republic of China

Guarantee
We cannot guarantee the following:

1. That the portraits will bear any resemblance to Mr Squitt or his lady wife.

2. That the mugs are not made by children below the age of 12 in conditions of near slavery.

3. That your mug will ever reach you.

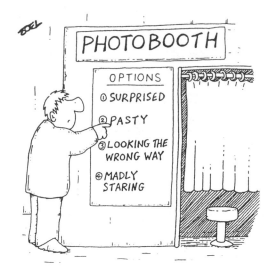

HAGUE NAMES NEW TEAM

by Our Westminster Staff **Lunchtime O'No-I-Said-It-Would-Be-Clarke**

WILLIAM HAGUE, the youngest Tory leader since Tony Blair, last night announced what he called "a fresh new look to the Shadow Cabinet".

Out go dull, tired old figures like Peter Lilley, Michael Howard, John Redwood and Dr Brian Mawhinney. In come exciting new faces like Peter Lilley, Michael Howard, John Redwood and Dr Brian Mawhinney.

And Hague has gone even further in his desire for "a new broom to inject some fresh blood into the hot potato of the Conservative party".

This is his exciting Shadow Cabinet:

● In as Chairman of the party comes the youthful 98 year old wunderkind **Cecil Parkinson**. His job will be to try and stand up.

● In as Lord Chancellor comes **Lord Hailsham**, 132, who aims to bring both his experience and his zimmer frame to the Shadow Cabinet.

● In as Minister for the Armed Forces comes the late **Sir Winston Churchill**, 160. Though dead he will bring "a real breath of new life to the party" says Hague.

● The **Duke of Wellington**, 231, is to be Shadow Foreign Minister. A known Eurosceptic and victor of Waterloo, his ashes will sit at the next EC summit on the Maastricht convergence criteria.

● **Boadicea**, who looks not a day older than her 1,873 years, was the former MP for Iceni North (later to become Finchley South after boundary changes). She will be joining Hague's team as an advisor on policy and will tell the Prime Minister exactly what to do.

Hague told reporters afterwards: "This team is sending out a very strong message. We are the opposition party of the future."

Mendelssohn Behaving Badly

Book of the Month

The Portrait of Dorian Hague

by Oscar Wilde

A CHILLING tale of an elderly man who looks old, tired and clapped out. Years of promises and betrayals, compromises and evasions, fudges and failures are etched onto his sinister face. He looks every inch of 87 years old.

Yet, in his attic, he has a terrible secret. It is a portrait of a fresh-faced young man of 36 who has no experience and is far too young to be leader of the Conservative Party.

As every day goes by, the portrait looks more immature — but the face of Dorian Hague looks more gaunt, grey and unelectable.

WARNING
Not suitable for adults

© Oscar Fry

BLAIR'S ASTONISHING AMSTERDAM TRIUMPH

by Our Political Staff **Alistair Campbell** (as dictated to all newspapers)

TONY Blair yesterday pulled off one of the most astounding political coups since Hannibal invaded the Alps *(writes Alistair Campbell, the man they can't gag)*.

From the land of tulips and windmills came the news that Tony had signed the treaty that makes Magna Carta look like a menu from McDonalds *(writes Alistair Campbell, the man who tells it like it isn't)*.

Here are just some of the astonishing victories that Tony won after two days and nights of hand-to-hand combat with some of the most ruthless political gangsters the world has seen since Genghis Khan put one over Al Capone in the first round *(writes Al Campbell, the politician the pundits ring up when they want to be told what to say)*.

● Britain to keep right to drive on left until 2005.
● A last-minute reprieve for London's famous red buses.
● English to remain official language of Great Britain "for foreseeable future".
● Postponement of EU's compulsory shopping-trolley driving test until 2007.
● Britain to keep 50% of the Single European Fish.
● Britain's prime minister to be allowed to win humorous bicycle race in return for signing the Social Chapter.

No wonder (writes Alistair Campbell) the rest of Europe were last night reeling in admiration at the man they are calling "El Pushover" *(surely 'the Iron Man of Islington'? Ed)*

London Underground Map

The Labour Line

UNDERGROUND

No Sell-Off

KEY ———

Labour Line
(formerly Tory Line)

Sell-Off

COURT AND SOCIAL

MARRIAGE

The marriage took place on Wednesday 18 June at St Margaret's, Westminster, of Mr Kenneth Clarke, son of the late Sir Edward Heath RN, and Mr John Vulcan, son of Krrrgx and Thrztp from the planet Redwood. The Chief Bridesmaid was Ms Teresa Gorperson, HRT. Monsignor Archie Hamilton officiated, and there was a reception afterwards on St Stephen's Green for the world's media. The ceremony was interrupted when an elderly woman was removed from the congregation screaming, "Don't be vague, ask for me!" The divorce took place the following day at 5.15 pm. William Hague was named as co-respondent.

HAGUE'S NEW FIANCÉE

We are very much in love

PATTEN WEEPS AS LAST POST SOUNDS AS HEAVENS OPEN AS BRITANNIA SAILS AS FLAG IS LOWERED AS EMPIRE COMES TO END — AND I WAS THERE!

 by **Lunchtime O'Boo-Hoo-Hoos**

IT WAS as though the heavens themselves were weeping as the band of the Royal Scots Hussars played "Abide With Me" for the last time in a monsoon-like downpour.

High on the peak of Mount Victoria a lone bagpiper sounded the Last Post while the biggest firework display the world has ever seen lit up the famous skyscraper-lined harbour of the phenomenon known simply as Hong Kong.

At exactly midnight the curtain came down on 147 years of history... opium wars... Prince Charles... junks sailing serenely... tower blocks... end of Empire... sense of foreboding... heads held high... Prince Charles... map of world marked red... Britannia sinks below waves... last Imperial pageant... fleetsh lit up... Tim Henman through to fourth round... is this enough?

© All newspapers.

THE PATTEN GIRLS

Posh Patten   **Sexy Patten**   **Baby Patten**

END OF ERA AS HACKS ROLL IN

by Our Freebie Staff **Dominic Largeone, Charles Mooreplease, Alan Freebisher, Max Hasdrinks and Simon Junket**

THE WORLD watched in dismay as thousands of hacks rolled over the border into Hong Kong to mark the handover of huge amounts of drink to the biggest army of reporters ever seen.

The citizens of Hong Kong stood open-mouthed in shock as wave after wave of hacks swept through the town, occupying all the bars and hotels in a matter of minutes.

"You would have thought they would have shown more restraint," said one terrified local cab driver, Mr Rickshaw Littlejohn.

"It's an invasion, that's what it is. Once they've had a few drinks they'll be round there interrogating me and asking me about the future.

"I had that Chris Patten's dog in the back of the cab once — very tasty it was too."

Everywhere it was the same story — the chilling sound of corks popping, and hacks barking orders at the cowed locals, such as "Trebles all round, matey — it's OK, it's all on Conrad."

There was no escape. Everywhere you looked there were men clutching mobile phones and shouting "Hold the front page! It's the Editor here — I've got a great scoop on what a brilliant party I've just been to."

And as the drinks were lowered (continued page 94)

Bill Deedes Writes

When I first came to Hong Kong for the old Morning Post in 1895, things were pretty different, I can tell you. I was only a young man of 60, just starting on life as a cub reporter... continued age 94.

Letters to the Editor

The Hong Kong Handover

SIR — I am sure all your readers were as shocked as I was by the pitiful behaviour of the self-styled "Governor of Hong Kong", Mr "Chris" Patten, during the handing over of our last remaining colony to the Communists.

Day after day we saw him on television blubbering and snivelling like some homesick schoolboy on the first day of term.

Whatever became of the stiff upper lip that was for so long the hallmark of the Englishman? No wonder the Chinese were jubilant as they goose-stepped down Kowloon High Street. No wonder they were openly contemptuous of the whimpering Patten as he cravenly pulled down the flag and handed over "The Jewel in the Crown" (which, I am delighted to say, is being reshown on Sunday evenings, with the delectable Miss Geraldine James playing the part previously played by herself. But I digress).

As one who has been out east and knows the wily ways of the Chinee, I can safely say that nothing could have been better calculated to convince the people of Hong Kong of the sad moral decline of our once-great nation than the spectacle of Mr Patten's pathetic lack of self-control as he sobbed helplessly into his suit. It was indeed hard to believe that this hapless cry-baby and bed-wetter was really a Governor in the same mould as, say, my late great-uncle, Sir Reginald Massingberd-Gussett, VC and Bar, who for 50 years served as Governor of the Gilbert and Sullivan Islands and handed them back to their inhabitants without a flicker of emotion as, clad only in his ostrich feathers, he rode his bicycle into the pitiless breakers of the Pacific Ocean and was lost forever. The very thought of it brings tears to my eyes. I must break off now to have a good manly weep.

SIR H. GUSSETT
Dunrulin, Jardine St Mathieson, Kowlooni, Nr Henley

Trial By Media

SIR — As one who has known Mr Iscariot for many years, may I say how I utterly deplore the recent pillorying he has received at the hands of certain sections of the media, who have both engineered and then gloated shamelessly over his downfall. Here was a young man of enormous ability and great personal charm, destined for the highest offices in the land, whose only real crime was to be well-born, handsome and rich. It was this that excited the envy of loathsome journalists, who hunted him down with all the pitiless savagery of a pack of hounds tearing to pieces some noble stag in the foothills of Ben Hebron.

If Mr Iscariot did receive the thirty pieces of silver alleged by the gutter press, then I have no doubt that there is a perfectly innocent explanation. It may well be that Mr Iscariot's wife was meant to pick up the money and take it to Switzerland, to donate it to a charity of her choice. Alternatively, those of us familiar with the workings of the security services know that it is often necessary to stay in the Paris Ritz, at the expense of some dodgy Arab, for the good of one's country.

Alternatively, I am completely off my head, which is the most likely explanation.

SAUL JOHNSON
c/o The Spectator

Wimbledon '97

PUNMANIA SWEEPS BRITAIN

by Our Tennis Staff **Phil Space**

YES! It's Wimbledon 1997 and the whole nation's gone PUN-CRAZY as British Punsters prove that they are the best in the world!

First-class English puns are once again making us proud. Puns such as: "Tim Gentleman Please!", "The Henman Cometh!", "Hendoubtedly the Greatest!", "Wimbledon Champi-Hen", "Tim Nice But Win", "Hen's Eggs-actly Perfect" and "Sampras Wins Wimbledon Again" *(surely 'Timbledon's Coming Hen!'? Ed.)*.

For years Britain's puns have been languishing in the outside pages, but now they have battled through every section and are now triumphantly on the centre of the front page.

International news hasn't a chance! No more German, French, American and Chinese stories! From now on Britain is Number Pun for desperate tennis-based humour!

ON OTHER PAGES:

(That's enough, Ed.)

Remember there's more Fun in the Pun!

SHOULD ANN WIDDECOMBE MARRY?

Charles Windsor writes

"ER... Well, you... just because she is an older woman and not very attractive... er... that doesn't mean that you know there is any constitutional reason why she shouldn't you know... as my old friend Sir Laurens van der Post used to say, 'As time goes by/The fundamental things apply/di dum di dum di dum'... and it's awfully true, isn't it?... Just because Ms Widdecombe has blotted her copybook, you know, been an MP and everything... that's not to say she shouldn't use her position as an unmarried single non-mother to lecture everyone about whatever she wants... er... It is a tricky one, isn't it?"

© Prince Charles.

CHARLES WEDDING SHOCK

Will you marry me?

We're not all gay, you know

"Good Heavens, Lucinda – it's a streaker"

WORLD'S FIRST NUDE VIOLINIST

'Not a gimmick' says promoter

by Our Classical Music Staff **Sir Henry Kelly, FM**

THE MANAGER of the sensational new 19-year-old performer from Scandinavia, Miss Linda Söftpørn, last night denied allegations that his protegee was being cynically marketed as a classical musician rather than as "a blonde with no clothes on".

Said Len Filth of the promoters, The Really Filthy Company: "Linda is a first-rate raunchy babe who just happens to play the violin to concert level. She would be a star without the violin and it is unfair to say that it has helped her in the serious business of getting her kit off."

Skinlandia

Miss Söftpørn has already recorded her first CD, entitled "For CD Men", which features the talented blonde taking off her clothes whilst incidentally playing some of the world's most beautiful music.

She has also been acclaimed by world-famous musical expert Lord Andrew Lloyd-Webber: "Don't be fooled by the classical music," said Lloyd-Website. "This is an internationally recognised naked lady at work."

WHAT YOU WILL HEAR

● Beethoven's Violin Concerto *(takes off dress)*

● Mendelssohn's Violin Concerto *(takes off Brahms. Shome mishtake shurely?)*

● Air on a G-String *(takes off money to the bank)*

Special video version available in Brown Paper Bag or visit Linda's website at www.violinporn.phworr.co.uk

"That's a nasty ingrowing toenail, Mr Kite — have you considered euthanasia?"

THAT EARTH SUMMIT ON THE ENVIRONMENT

Delegates' Agenda in Full

1. Fly across globe to New York in half-empty jumbo jet.
2. Take large stretch limousine from airport to conference centre.
3. Turn on in-car air-conditioning during 6-hour traffic jam.
4. Fill up 30-gallon tank with petrol every 2 miles.
5. Issue 19 million communiques on the subject of deforestation.
6. Play friendly round of golf on course (formerly nature reserve).
7. Fly in helicopter back to the airport to avoid traffic.
8. Get held in stack above JFK.
9. Miss jumbo jet flight and take Concorde (as only passenger).
10. Buy duty-free cigarettes for everyone at the office.

© *Society for the Protection of Endangered Conferences*

"Well, go back to South America and see if I care!"

NAOMI TOOK 'HUGE OVERDOSE' SHOCK

by Our Medical Staff

THE world-famous model Miss Naomi Campbell, 22, took a huge overdose of publicity yesterday, according to sources close to her agent.

"From what we gather, she had 300 front pages followed by a couple of thousand stories later on the same day.

"It was critical," continued the source, "but she is now out of danger of being forgotten."

Joaquin Cortes is 93.

ULSTER 'APPEALS FOR CALM' AS MURDERING SEASON BEGINS

by Our Norther Ireland Staff **Lunchtime O'Boyne**

THERE were renewed fears that Ulster might be in for a "long, hot summer" as the traditional murdering season once again got under way last night in all parts of the province.

For reasons now so far lost in history that no one can remember what they are, representatives of Ulster's two communities affirm their traditional identities by parading through the streets and murdering each other.

Armageddon

Although many observers feel that these murders are an integral and colourful part of the province's rich heritage, in recent years there have been increasingly vocal calls for these rituals to be banned.

"These murders do very little to promote harmony between Protestants and Catholics," said a member of the Royal Ulster Constabulary yesterday, shortly before he himself became a victim of traditional gunshots from both sides simultaneously.

Despite the recent campaign to outlaw the murders, however, it seems that this tradition is still enjoyed by too many people for them to be abandoned.

The next flashpoint is likely to be tomorrow, when the funerals take place of last week's victims *(continued for ever)*

That Blair – Clinton Dinner Menu in full

SIR TERENCE CONRAN'S LE PONT DE LA TOUR

Waffle and syrup   £500.00

❖ ❖ ❖

Service not included

CLINTON FLIES IN

I'm going to talk to your Cabinet

Good idea. I must try it myself

The Spice Girls CBE

Lord Wallace of Gromit

Sir Timothy Henman

NEW POPULAR BIRTHDAY HONOURS

Honours in full *(cont from p. 49)*

for services to HMSO (Sudbury); **Ms P.F.B. Mildington-Furrows**, Chief Supervisor, Internal Post and Communications, The Treasury; **Mr S.R.L. Hubcap**, Official Chauffeur to the Secretary of the Board of Trade.

DHL (Colonies)

J.M.B. Alcopop, Head of the Island Bus Company, St Bruno's; **R.R. Frangipani**, Chief Surveyor, Department of the Interior, Bountibar; **Mrs F.C. Goodi-Goodi** Gummadrop, Warden of the Turtle Sanctuary, The Euston Archipelago.

KC (and the Sunshine Band)

Sir William Wonker, 2nd Commercial Secretary to the Woodwind Islands Trade Mission (1965-66); **Sir Trevor Trumpet-Smythe**, Assistant Acting Permanent Secretary to the Antarctic Federation (Munich); **Lady Petronella Umbrella**, Personal Private Secretary to his Excellency the Mardi of Gras; **Mrs N.Y.P.D. Blue**, the *(continued page 94)*

Lord Papa and Lady Nicole of Renault

The Teletubbies, Companions of Honour

Sir Donald Sinden *(surely shome mistake? Ed)*

"Amazing! We still get mail for them, and they left years ago"

FAT OLD VOLCANO BLOWS TOP

by Our Man In The West Indies
Ferdinand Mountserrat

AN elderly volcano, long thought to be extinct, yesterday erupted, spewing out huge clouds of poisonous gas.

A continuous stream of black bile poured in the direction of Mr William Hague, an innocent teenager who through no fault of his own had become leader of the Conservative Party.

The dreaded Mount Heath, which has spluttered intermittently for years, finally exploded when the internal pressure of seeing someone else become leader of the party became too great to bear.

Lava-Tory

Although badly shaken by the tide of filth which had engulfed him, staining his blazer and shorts, the diminutive Mr Squitt promised to be back at school in time for his exams *(surely 'wedding'? Ed.)*.

Mount Grocer is 278.

Letters to the Editor

From Sir Herbert Gusset

SIR—Like many of your readers, it was recently my honour and privilege to travel up to London to take part in the wonderful and inspiring "Rally" in support of traditional country pursuits, such as fox-hunting, skittle-baiting and mole-coursing, of the last of which I personally have been a lifelong devotee. Indeed, for a brief period back in the late 1940s I was honoured to be chosen as "Master Moler" of the Mendip and District Molehunt. But I digress.

On arriving at the capital for the great "Demonstration", I stopped off once or twice to fortify myself for the long march ahead. And soon I was being carried along by a convivial crowd of fellow countryfolk, clad gaily in dark glasses, black leather trousers and heavy boots, towards the park which was our destination.

"Are you one of us?" enquired a young yeoman, with pink hair and a large droopy moustache. "Indeed I am, sir," I replied, "and proud to be so."

At which, I confess, I was rather surprised when he kissed me on the lips and invited me to his cottage in Hornsey.

Such was the euphoria in which we were all caught up, that I did not hear any of the speeches from such well-known champions of country pursuits as Sir Nicholas Soames, Mr Michael Heseltine and Mr Auberon Waugh. But I was delighted to see how many young people were prepared to travel up from every corner of the land to make clear their views, or as one militant young lady put it, "Come out of the closet".

I would just like to congratulate those responsible for this splendid occasion on a superb feat of organisation. They had even had the forethought to provide thousands of toilets — at least one for every two demonstrators. With support like this, no wonder Johnny Fox is quaking in his boots.

SIR H. GUSSETT
"Tally-Ho", Clapham Common

"He's always got to go one better than the other lion-tamers"

SCIENTISTS BAFFLED BY 'HUGE FLAT ROCKS' ON MARS

by Our Science Staff **Adams Mars-Jones**

NASA boffins admitted last night that they were mystified by the mysterious plateau-like formations that seem to litter the otherwise barren surface of Mars.

"What we have here," said one puzzled planet-watcher, "are symmetrical piles of carbon-based matter stacked in rows thousands of miles high and millions of miles wide.

Relaunch Rocket

"It is a truly awesome sight — but, incredible as it may seem, there are discernible signs of lettering on the piles and there are even what look like drawings."

The space telescope on the Mars Rover appears to show a crude image of an alien coming out of a spaceship and asking a sheep to "take me to your leader", with the signature of "Mahood" in the corner.

Scientists are already dubbing these huge formations "unsold copies of Punch magazine" and their sites appear on the maps marked as the Valley of Al-Fayed.

The Unread Planet

But the scientists deny that this discovery proves there is intelligent life on Mars. A man with a beard told reporters:

"The magazine may have existed millions of years ago but it is now clearly dead. It could not survive on Mars, but then it could not survive on Earth".

ON OTHER PAGES: Colour pictures of girls with no clothes on.

THE INVISIBLE MAN | MEETS A LADY

The Daily Hurleygraph

NEWSPAPER OF THE YEAR

Friday, July 25, 1997

Versace shot World mourns

by Our Fashion Staff
CHRISTOPHER VOGUE
Miami, Tuesday

THE WORLD was in total shock last night following the news that a man who once designed a dress for the international megastar Liz Hurley had been gunned down by a gay serial killer.

Tributes to the late Allegro Vivace poured in from the four corners of the earth.

Among those to mourn the genius they called "the man who once designed a dress for Liz Hurley" were: Elton John, Ben Elton, the late Augustus John, Tony Benn, Mother Teresa, the late Leonid Brezhnev, the Spice Girls and the late Sir Edward Heath.

That Dress

In a long and illustrious career that lasted well over two years, Vivace left his stamp on the 20th century like few other artists.

But undoubtedly his most lasting achievement was the astonishing creation in black and gold in which Liz Hurley attended the world premiere of the award-winning film *Four*

Safety Pins And A Piece Of Cloth.
Fashion guru Alexandra Schoolmarm held back her tears last night to explain that "Vivace was a god to all who knew him. He was Leonardo da Vinci,

Picasso and the Beatles all rolled into one.

"He was the first person to realise that people without any taste would buy his clothes for a lot of money."

Inside

Is there intelligent life on Ulster?

Our Science Staff investigates

THE "Orange Planet", as it is called, has long been assumed to be a barren wasteland incapable of supporting any civilisation, but earlier this year there were a few optimistic signs of sentient life forms on the planet.

However, when the new probe, the Mo Mowlam, was finally released onto the surface, there was nothing to be seen except huge explosions going off on all sides, with clouds of gas and smoke rising into the hostile atmosphere.

The data initially coming from the Mowlam indicated "little orange men" moving along in formation with curiously shaped black heads and then "little green men" appearing and throwing projectiles at them.

Scientists, however, were unimpressed. "We have seen this sort of thing before on Ulster. It has been going on for millions of years and it means nothing. There is no reason for anyone to raise their hopes about the future of the planet." *(Surely 'province'? Ed.)*

QUEEN MOTHER TO BE RELAUNCHED BY PRIVATE ENTERPRISE

By **Victoria Britannia**

ONE of Britain's proudest Royal possessions, Her Majesty Queen Elizabeth the Queen Mother, is to be refitted and leased out to private companies for promotional and recretional purposes.

Said a spokesman: "She has been a symbol of Britain for nearly a century but the cost of keeping her afloat is prohibitive in today's market economy."

He continued: "What we are proposing is a viable leaseback timeshare option where the Queen Mother is available for corporate hospitality both here and abroad.

"A number of companies have already expressed interest in purchasing a share of the Queen Mother, including Gordon's, Beefeater, Gilbey's, Ladbrokes, William Hill, Cadburys and Hats'n'Handbags'R'Us of Beauchamp Place.

POETRY CORNER

In Memoriam: Terry Nation, Creator of the Daleks

So. Farewell then
Terry Nation.

Creator of the
Daleks.

Now you
Have been
Exterminated.

No disrespect
Intended.

E.J. Thribb (17½)

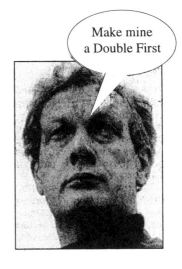

In Memoriam: Lines written on the departure from Oxford University of Professor Norman Stone for the Mehmet Thatcher Historical Institute, Ankara

Sho. Farewell then
Professor Shtone.
You have been
Shacked.

Thish callsh for
A drink.
Ash you would
Shay.

E.J. Thribb (aged 17½)

In Memoriam: Allen Ginsberg

So. Farewell
Then Allen
Ginsberg.

"I saw the
Best minds of my
Generation destroyed
By madness, starving
Hysterical naked,
Dragging themselves
Through the negro
Streets at dawn
Looking for an
Angry fix."

Yes. That
Was your
Catchphrase.

You were a
Beat Poet.

Now you
Are a
Dead Beat Poet.

So no
Change there
Then.

E.J. Thribbsberg (71½)

In Memoriam: Lines On The Sacking Of Sir Peregrine Worsthorne, Senior Columnist And Former Editor Of The Sunday Telegraph

So. Farewell
Then. Sir Peregrine
Worsthorne.

You have been
Sacked after 30
Years of loyal
Service to the
Sunday Telegraph.

"The free
Market". That
Was your
Catchphrase.

Now you know
What it
Means.

E.J. Thribb (17½)
Winner of the T.S. Eliot Prize for his slim
volume *A Garland of Withered Leaves*

WORLD'S MOST GLAMOROUS MONEY-MAKER DIES

by Our City Staff **Lazlo Goldfinger**

THE world of finance was in mourning last night for one of the world's greatest and most glamorous money makers, Sir Jiammi Verspasta.

Jiammi's creations were world renowned. His collections of money, made from all the world's leading currencies in different parts of the world, rendered him a household name. Women everywhere wanted to be seen with his money — the familiar dollar bill, the dazzling deutschmark, the exotic Mexican peso.

NOW! Man Dead

Tributes trickled in last night from the world of cash. Said fellow multi-millionaire Taki Cocupthenos: "He was an example to us all. A man of outstanding wealth with a brilliant bank balance and a wonderful way with dosh."

Former City whizz-kid Jim

Slater saluted his old friend: "Whatever else you said about him, you had to admire his money. He had much more of it than me. I don't think I have met anyone who had as much."

Said another friend and admirer, Conrad Black: "He was a creative genius when it came to money. He used it in a way that no one had ever done before. Of course he was vulgar and obscene. But that was Jiammi. We shall not see his like again."

Gnome

IT is with great sorrow and regret that I pen this brief and inadequate tribute to one of the greatest men of our times — my old friend, Sir James Goldsmith.

Although he amassed a huge fortune, he was more than just a mere financier. He had a brilliant mind and was widely read, with a library of over 2 million books.

Despite his wealth he never lost touch with ordinary people, many of whom he liberated from the tyranny of employment. Others, like the humble peasants on his Mexican scorpion farm, he deprived of their livelihood.

Later, when he turned to politics, he showed here again his famed Marmite touch, helping his beloved Conservative Party to an overwhelming and glorious defeat at the polls.

Our heartfelt sympathies at this time go out to his hundreds of wives, mistresses, love children, and in particular to his faithful libel lawyer Mr Carter-Ruck, who finds himself cruelly bereaved of his most valuable client.

E. Strobes
pp Lord Gnome
Marmite House
Port Talbot
Mexico

CAMBRIDGE 'WOMAN DON' WAS MAN SHOCK

by Our Academic Staff **Henry Porterhouse-Bluestocking**

THE WORLD of scholarship was rocked to its foundations yesterday when it was revealed that a prominent woman lecturer at an all-female college was in fact a man.

Dr "Germaine" Greer, an English professor, had attracted suspicion for some time by her overtly masculine behaviour.

Said a shocked colleague, Dr Hilary Term: "Some of us were worried by Dr Greer's behaviour, which did not seem at all in keeping with that expected of a female don.

Don't Be Beastly To The Germaines

"She was aggressive and foul-mouthed, peppering her lectures with four-letter words and obscenities, and boasting of her sexual exploits.

"She behaved to other women like a typical male chauvinist, commenting on their appearance in a derogatory and sexist manner."

One woman who fell foul of Dr Greer's contempt for her supposed sex was a female journalist, savaged for her "bird's nest hair", "fat cleavage" and "fuck me shoes".

Silly Punt

But the college authorities have now learned that Dr Greer's real name is Clive James, an Australian who came to England in the 1960s to pursue an academic career.

After undergoing a sex-change operation in the 1970s, Mr James transformed himself into Dame Edna Everage, the so-called "female eunuch".

Prof. Rolfina Harris is 97.

"Hmm, Nordic, but nice"

McHANSARD
What you will see

SCOTTISH PARLIAMENTARY DEBATES

3pm. 1st Reading of the Bill to Outlaw the Propagation of Defamatory Rumour Amongst Parliamentarians.

Angus McGrotty (Gorbals, Lab): I would just like to point out that my honourable friend, the member for Shallowgrave is a poof! *(Cries of "Shame on ye!", "Gang awae!" and "We all thought so")*

Rhona McNasty (Trainspotting, Lab): I wonder how much money my honourable friend was paid by the drug barons of Dundee to say that! *(Cries of "Shame on ye!", "Gang awae!" and "Can we have some money too?")*

The Speaker (Mrs McBoothroyd): Order, order, I must ask honourable members to remember that the eyes of the world will be judging us by our actions here today. *(Cries of "Shaddup, ya old slag!")*

Archie McSleazy (Meldrew, Lab): May I just bring to the house's notice the fact that one cannot go into a toilet in the parliament building without being given AIDS by some drunken, sexually degenerate wife-beater. I should like to know how much money these honourable members are prepared to pay me to keep quiet in future debates.

The Speaker (Mrs McPhone-Booth): I have an important announcement to make. The members bar is now open. *(House empties to cheers and cries of "Let me through, I'm a Scottish MP")*

THAT TORY 'BONDING' WEEKEND IN FULL

by Our Political Staff **Sid and Boris Johnson**

THE following top-secret memo has been leaked to Private Eye by a highly placed source within Tory Central Office.

It sets out in stark detail Tory leader William Hague's top-secret plan to revitalise his ailing party, and to win the next election by a Blair-style landslide.

CONSERVATIVE CENTRAL OFFICE SMITH SQUARE, SW1

To: All Conservative Members of Parliament (For Your Eyes Only)
From: W. Hague, Team Leader

Day One

0930 hrs. Assemble in reception of Thorneycroft Country Hotel, Aylesbury, Bucks.

0940 hrs. Goals and Visions: Seminar led by Simon Kumquat, Project Director, ASDA Supermarket Group.

1100 hrs. Coffee and Biscuits.

1115 hrs. The Mission Statement. Liz Yoghurt, Marketing Director Yog-U-Like (UK), defines the parameters of building a viable corporate identity.

1200-1500 hrs. Buffet Lunch.

1500 hrs. Problem-Solving Exercise with Lt-Col Philip de Nutter of the Parachute Regiment. Teams will be required to cross an imaginary river, using only a copy of the Daily Telegraph and a box of matches.

1600 hrs. Team-Building Line Dancing with "Big Tex" Homecare of the Texas Homecare Dance Experience (Basingstoke).

1700 hrs. The Day So Far. MPs will split into focus groups to engage in frank assessment of the effectiveness of the training sessions to date, led by Dick Swatch, managing director of management consultants Swatch Switch.

1800 hrs. MPs go into bar to get pissed and discuss what a waste of time the whole day has been and what a hopeless squit Hague is. *(Surely some mistake? Ed.)*

LONDON BELONGS TO ME

A **GODFREY BOWMAN** Adventure
by Masterstoryteller **JEFFREY ARCHER**

FROM his penthouse flat looking out over the world-famous River Thames, the svelte, sun-tanned, handsome, Savile-Row-suited, very rich figure of Godfrey Bowman gazed down over the heart of England's capital city, London.

From Hammersmith in the East to Tower Bridge way out to the West, the story was the same.

Three long months of Socialist rule had reduced the world's greatest city to a seedy, rat-infested slum.

How very different from the £2 million view of the Post Office Tower by the world-famous French artist Gustave Monet, which hung in place of honour above the leather-bound set of first editions of Bowman's own best-selling novels.

In the streets below him the new cries of London could be heard — "Can you spare some change, guv?", "Buy a Big Issue, Mister?", "Is this the way to Shepherds Market?"

The people of London had never known such a dark time since the famous Blitz of 1948 or the Great Plague of 1923 *(please check)*.

And now, it seemed, final disaster threatened.

An unscrupulous Communist politician, known to his followers as 'Red Ken', was said to be back in town, plotting revolution.

It wouldn't be long before the once-proud city fell under the brutal heel of this fanatical Socialist dictator, known for his charming habit of torturing his collection of pet newts.

It was a nightmare vision…

"IT IS a nightmare vision, Lord Bowman. And there is only one man in my kingdom who can avert catastrophe."

"Who is that speaking?" Bowman barked.

"It is Her Majesty the Queen, Lord Bowman. And I have a mission for you."

"At your service, Ma'am," purred Bowman, flexing his SAS-trained muscles in readiness to carry out the regal command.

His loyalty was absolute, drummed into him by long years on the playing fields of Eton, the quadrangles of Oxbridge University and at Sandhurst, where he had passed out with the Sword of Honour in the same year that he won the 100 Metres Gold Medal for Britain at the Olympic Games.

"Your great achievements for this country are not forgotten," said the Queen, as if reading his thoughts.

"But now an even greater task awaits you. Turn again, Bowman, Lord Mayor of London…"

THE BELLS of St Paul's Abbey were ringing out. They could be heard from Muswell Hill in the South to Tooting Bec in the North. Never had so many Londoners jammed the streets of their beloved City, to cheer one man as he emerged on the balcony of Buckingham House, Her Majesty the Queen radiant at his side.

The Red Arrows display team flashed overhead, leaving a purple smoke trail which proclaimed the joyous message: VIVAT BOWMAN — THE PEOPLE'S MAYOR.

Few people noticed the Black Maria threading its way slowly through the throng.

Cowering in the back was the pitiful moustachioed figure of Red Ken, the hated Stalinist traitor, as he was driven to lifelong incarceration in the famous Tower of Windsor.

The crowd roared their delight, for they knew their city was saved.

© Lord Archole of Weston-super-Toseeyou

"This is the secure ward for men who argue with radios"

RADIO BORE

The Today Programme

Jim Naughtie: And now the national and international news with Brian Perkins.

Perky: Easily the most important thing happening in the world today will be the announcement by Mr James Boyle of the radical changes in the Radio 4 schedule. Details of the changes have been kept a closely guarded secret, but the BBC has learned that the changes will be announced to the nation by Mr Boyle at 10.15 this morning.

Mr Boyle's announcement will bring to an end months of fevered speculation which has had the entire country talking about very little else.

Among the main questions to be answered by Mr Boyle, the head of Radio 4, will be whether the *Today* programme should begin earlier; whether *Does He Take Sugar?* is to be moved to a new afternoon slot; whether the five-minutes-to-two shipping forecast will be moved to 3.35; and whether the long-running *Call Ed Stourton Show* is to be axed altogether.

An extended exclusive interview with Mr Boyle will be broadcast immediately after this news.

And now the rest of the news. In Israel thousands died when some bomb went off. Some blonde woman seems to have murdered someone. The New Labour government is up to various things. And half of Germany seems to have disappeared underwater.

Naughtiebutnice: And now we are very privileged to have in the studio my boss, Mr James Bore. Mr Bore, can you tell us what it is you're going to announce to the world later this morning about your radical plans for New Radio 4?

Bore: Certainly not. It would be quite improper for me to pre-empt my own very important announcement by telling Radio 4 listeners what is going to happen to their programmes.

Naughtiebutnotquitesonice: But is it true to say that what you are planning is a "dumbing-down" of Radio Four?

Bore: How dare you use such a tasteless and inaccurate term to describe my innovative and frankly brilliant decision to shift the lunchtime *Archers* to 2 o'clock? One more question like that and you're fired.

Naughtiebutsuddenlysweetaspie: Gosh, sir, I'm sorry. Thank you very much for coming in. It has been a great honour to have you on the show. And now *Thought for the Day* from the Rt. Rev. Jim Wheelbarrow, Bishop of Neasden.

Wheelbarrow: You know, when we hear of all these amazing changes at Radio 4, don't we all think: "Oh dear, I'm not sure about this"? But then we have a little pause for reflection. And we realise that change is always painful. And in the end we realise that it is the right thing after all, and we're very grateful that we've been shaken out of our old complacency.

Humphrys: Thank you, Bishop Jim. And now a summary of the news from Brian Perky.

Pinky: In an extraordinary interview on this programme, the man at the centre of the world's most important news story exclusively revealed that he was unable to say anything at all...

(This continues for several hours until finally, at 10.15am, a man in a suit and glasses announces some minor adjustments to the scheduling of Woman's Hour and the format of the Melvyn Barg Talk Show...)

Later on The World at One

Nick Clarke: And now we are going over live for an exclusive interview with the world's most famous and important man, Mr James Bore.

Bore: Look, you see, all the press were wrong. I didn't sack Alastair Cooke, I did move the time of the *Morning Service* and I haven't made a decision on *Yesterday in Parliament.*

That just shows how stupid all the journalists are.

Clarke: And how clever you are?

Bore: Precisely. I've commissioned a huge amount of research through focus groups and deliberative polling, to discover why so many people switch off Radio Four at about 9 o'clock in the morning and don't switch on again until around 6pm.

Clarke: It's because they go to work, isn't it?

Bore: You're fired.

Other programmes on today's Radio 4

Sport On Four: Cliff Morgan interviews David Gower about the new changes to Radio 4.

The Archers: Conversation at the Bull turns to the big talking point of the moment, the radical changes down at Radio 4 and the move of Farming Today from 6.10am to 5.51am.

Book At Bedtime: James Bore reads extracts from his New Radio Four schedule and sends nation to sleep.

ROME CONSTRUCTION WORKS

WILL TAKE MORE THAN A DAY

New Foreign Office Ethical Guidelines

Part 94: Dealing with Uganda

Ugandan Affairs are extremely complicated and it is inappropriate to apply any hard and fast rules when dealing with this state. Negotiations should be conducted in camera (or in handy ministerial love nest close to the House of Commons), not on the front page of the *News of the World*.

Signed

Mr Robin Cock

We apologise for the mis-spelling of Mr Cock's name in the above article. It should of course have read 'Mr Fook'.

We apologise for the mis-spelling of Mr Fook's name in the above apology. It should of course have read Mr 'Cook-Up'. *(That's enough corrections. Ed)*

EXCLUSIVE PHOTO

THE most amazing picture ever taken is today proudly printed by The Mirror. And it is entirely genuine.

It shows the glamorous playboy editor, Piers Moron, with the new love of his life the beautiful press baron David Montgomery.

We can see from their body language that they are quite clearly in love and the tell-tale signs of physical affection announce to the world that this time it's for real.

Piers is kissing his reputation and his career goodbye.

The Mirror is proud to bring to its readers this tender and touched-up *(surely 'touching'? Ed.)* photograph.
© *The Moron.*

"We're not your real parents – actually you're a genetically modified tomato"

*"Usually the sex **stops** when the honeymoon is over"*

The CARNIVAL Collection

Casual Wear for the '90s from
Racing Gnome's Mail Order Catalogue

FOR HIM

❶ A cool, relaxed "Youngster" shirt* in trendy, stonewashed denim for that "weekend in Nottinghill look". **£7.90** ❷ Hand-stitched, full-length "Hipster" Chino-style slacks in washable Gnomeskin™. **£11.95**

*Colour Range: Blue

FOR HER

❸ Weekend-smart "Ffioncée" button-up blouse for the modern woman who's on her way up. **£2.99**
❹ Tropical, wrinkle-resistant "Clare Shorts" in 100% organic cotton give the garment that "worn-in look". **£8.60**

Chessmen Behaving Badly

POL JOHNSON FOUND

by Our Cambodia Staff **Lu Ne Binh**

A PATHETIC old man with white hair and a red face was put on show in the *Daily Mail* yesterday, after being tracked down in the dense verbiage of the *Spectator*.

Those who have seen him are convinced that he is the notorious Pol Johnson, the man who bored millions of people to death in the space of one afternoon.

Khmer Rouge Face

Now 85, Pol Potty became world-famous in the 1970s as one of the great mass-journalists of all time, often despatching up to 50,000 words in less than an hour.

A hard-line lunatic, Johnson was feared by all who opened a newspaper, and the public lived in terror of being confronted by one of his fearsome diatribes on the collapse of civilisation as we know it.

Today Pol's thoughts are confused and his mind rambles incoherently on any subject that comes into it.

As one long-time observer put it: "Nothing has changed."

Pol Potty is 106.

A Doctor writes

As a doctor I am often asked: "Why has your husband left you and run off with his secretary?".

Well, the simple answer is "I blame the Tories."

Due to the draconian cuts in NHS funding under the last government, or *Virginia bottomlensis thatcherium* to give it the full medical name, many senior doctors such as myself have to work such long hours that we never get a chance to spend time

at home with our husbands.

If you are worried about your husband, have a look in the News of the World and see if there is a picture of him with some young Labour researcher.

© *Dr Margaret Cook*

The Late Princess Diana

An Apology

IN recent weeks (not to mention the last ten years) we at the Daily Gnome, in common with all other newspapers, may have inadvertently conveyed the impression that the late Princess of Wales was in some way a neurotic, irresponsible and manipulative troublemaker who had repeatedly meddled in political matters that did not concern her and personally embarrassed Her Majesty The Queen by her Mediterranean love-romps with the son of a discredited Egyptian businessman.

We now realise as of Sunday morning that the Princess of Hearts was in fact the most saintly woman who has ever lived, who, with her charitable activities, brought hope and succour to hundreds and millions of people all over the world.

We would like to express our sincere and deepest hypocrisy to all our readers on this tragic day and hope and pray that they will carry on buying our paper notwithstanding.

© *The Daily Gnome*

DO NOT blame the Mirror for this tragic event. The sleazy foreign paparazzi are entirely different from the good honest British snappers who provide pictures for decent newspapers like the Mirror. These paparazzi are filth. They are frogs, wops and assorted spivs who will stop at nothing to get their disgusting pictures of our beloved British Royalty.

We at the Mirror would not stoop so low. We just buy the pictures from them.

Reproduced from the Sun with the name changed.

Candle In The Wind

by Our Royal Correspondent Phillipa Space

AS the candles flicker in the wind, like Diana's brief candle flickered in the wind of our lives, and the chill wind of mortality makes each of our candles flicker as the wind flickers *(Get on with it. Ed.)*, there is only one word that can convey the emotion that is in each of our hearts. Thank you. Thank you for saving the livelihoods of thousands of journalists and helping literally millions of copies walk out of the shops. *(Go back to the candles. Ed.)* And so the candle finally *(continued in all papers all week)*

HOUNDED TO DEATH BY THE WINDSORAZZI?

by Our Royal Staff **Phil Space**

WAS Diana a victim of the notorious Windsor rat pack who drove her to despair and forced her to leave the country by their continual acts of harassment.

"There is no one as ruthless as the Windsorazzi", said one Royal watcher, "when they get their prey in their sight. They may look harmless riding around on horses, but they will stop at nothing to get what they want."

"They wanted her out of the picture. And now they have got their way."

"He's made a killing on these pictures"

Highlights from the TV coverage

Sunday 3.17 p.m.

Martyn Lewis: ...so, you never met Diana but you must have some memories of her?

Man With Beard in Black Tie: I suppose my first reaction when I heard the news was one of shock and disbelief.

Martyn Lewis: So, your first reaction was one of shock and disbelief?

(Caption appears: "Dr Wilmot Pringle, former reader in Constitutional Studies, Strathclyde University")

Dr Pringle: Well, I er...

Martyn Lewis: Thank you for that, Dr Pringle, I am sure that all over the country viewers will be sharing your feelings of shock and disbelief. Now we've just heard that we can go over live to Balmoral...

Woman with microphone on windswept road: Well, Martyn, I am standing here on the windswept road where shortly the Royal car will arrive, possibly with the Queen and other members of the Royal Family on board, although we are not sure who will be with the Queen or if the Queen will actually come down this road to wherever it is she might be going.

Martyn Lewis: Well, thank you, Jenny. And it's not hard to imagine what the Queen must be feeling at this tragic and historic time, wherever she is. Now I am joined in the studio by Anthony Holden, David Mellor, Ben Pimlott, Jeffrey Archer, Richard Branson, Roy Jenkins, Jeffrey Archer, Jim Callaghan, Richard Branson, Anthony Holden and Jeffrey Archer. *(Men in black ties and suits look serious)*

Gentlemen, can I begin by asking you how you all felt when you were asked to come on this programme?

All: I suppose our first reaction was one of shock and disbelief since we have nothing worthwhile to say at all.

Martyn Lewis: Thank you, gentlemen, for your thoughts on this most tragic day. And we are now getting tributes from all over the world; the Life President of Rumbabwe has said in the last hour that his reaction to the news was one of "shock and disbelief on this most tragic day"; Dr Kissinger told reporters that he was shocked and disbelieving at the news on this most tragic day; and William Hague and Paddy Ashdown said that they were equally shocked and disbelieving as Tony Blair.

Now over to Los Angeles where Billy Connelly and Pamela Stephenson are *(continued for several weeks)*

The Englifh Civil War